P9-DDI-154

Further Praise for *Preparing the Ghost*

"Fans of Federico Fellini and, most especially, of Georges Perec will adore Mr. Frank's infuriatingly baroque, charmingly eccentric, and utterly unforgettable book. And with hand on heart I can truly say that I also loved every word of it."

—Simon Winchester, author of *The Professor and the Madman*

"The poets say there *is* another world—but it's in *this* one. Certainly that's the story of the giant squid, a story of secret darkness and secret wonder now unearthed (unoceaned?) by Matthew Gavin Frank, in prose so lusciously confected and allusively layered, I challenge you to randomly pick *any* ten pages from this book and not become mesmerized."

—Albert Goldbarth, author of *The Kitchen Sink: New and Selected Poems*

"*Preparing the Ghost* reads like a cross between Walt Whitman and a fever dream. Who would think squid and ice cream go together? I remained riveted to the very last word."

—Sy Montgomery, author of *The Good Good Pig: The Extraordinary Life of Christopher Hogwood*

"Matthew Gavin Frank reinvents the art of research in extraordinarily imaginative ways. His meditation on the briefly known and the forever unknowable courts lore (both family and creaturely), invites the fantastical, heeds fact, and turns the human drive to notate and list into a gesture of lyrical beauty."

—Lia Purpura, author of *On Looking* and *Rough Likeness*

"Matthew Gavin Frank has fashioned a book-length essay marked by unforeseen oneiric asides, and of real and imaginary escapades in search of one Newfoundlander's giant squid. *Preparing the Ghost* is a mash-up of a meditation on the nature of myth, the magnetic distance between preservation and perseverance, and the "sympathetic cravings" that undergird pain. In Frank's heart-thumping taxonomy, monstrous behemoths square nicely with butterflies and ice cream. Don't ask me how: read this book!"

—Mary Cappello, author of *Swallow: Foreign Bodies, Their Ingestion, Inspiration, and the Curious Doctor Who Extracted Them*

"What a marvelous essay Matthew Gavin Frank has written. *Preparing the Ghost* is driven by narrative, by lyric association, by memoir, by lists, by research, by imagination. Frank delivers this story of Moses Harvey, the first person to photograph the giant squid, with a passion as supercharged as Harvey's own. Above all, this is an essay about obsession, mystery, mythmaking, and the colossal size of our lives. Take it all in. Revel in its majesty."

—Lee Martin, author of *Such a Life*

"Like the giant squid at the center of this enchanting inquiry, Matthew Gavin Frank's *Preparing the Ghost* is a multi-tentacled and entirely captivating saga of profound mystery and relentless pursuit."

—Dinty W. Moore, author of *Between Panic & Desire*

"Part history, part lyric poem, part detective novel—Matthew Gavin Frank's *Preparing the Ghost* is just as intriguing and hard to classify as its subject. I never thought I'd care so much about the elusive giant squid, but thanks to this book, I can't help but see its shadow everywhere."

—Brenda Miller, author of *Listening Against the Stone*

"A great essay takes us into the author's polymathic mind and out to the wondrous world, teaching us something we didn't know we wanted to know. In *Preparing the Ghost*'s deliciously delirious layering of science, biography, history, mystery, linguistics, myth, philosophy, epistemology, adventure, and travel, Matthew Gavin Frank has given us a truly great essay."

—Partick Madden, author of *Quotidiana*

PREPARING THE GHOST

Also by Matthew Gavin Frank

Pot Farm

Barolo

The Morrow Plots

Warranty in Zulu

Sagittarius Agitprop

Preparing the Ghost

An Essay Concerning the Giant Squid and Its First Photographer

Matthew Gavin Frank

LIVERIGHT PUBLISHING CORPORATION

A Division of W. W. Norton & Company

New York • London

Printed in the United States of America
First Edition

For information about permission to reproduce selections from this book,
write to Permissions, W. W. Norton & Company, Inc.,
500 Fifth Avenue, New York, NY 10110

For information about special discounts for bulk purchases,
please contact W. W. Norton Special Sales at
specialsales@wwnorton.com or 800-233-4830

Manufacturing by Courier Westford
Book design by Ray Shappell
Production manager: Anna Oler

ISBN 978-0-87140-283-7

Liveright Publishing Corporation,
500 Fifth Avenue, New York, N.Y. 10110
www.wwnorton.com

W. W. Norton & Company Ltd.,
Castle House, 75/76 Wells Street, London W1T 3QT

1 2 3 4 5 6 7 8 9 0

For L, the Brookieface,
and so many other wonderful things

CONTENTS

AUTHOR'S NOTE xi

PART ONE:
The Largest Animal Without a Backbone 1

PART TWO:
The Mere Fabrications of a Distorted Mind 93

PART THREE:
All of These Suckers 127

PART FOUR:
We're Coming to a Head Wind 183

SOURCES 283

ACKNOWLEDGMENTS 295

AUTHOR'S NOTE

Though I've taken imaginative leaps with many scenes in this book, all quotations and historical facts, unless otherwise indicated, are as accurate as possible.

Part One

THE LARGEST ANIMAL WITHOUT A BACKBONE

THE CURTAINS WERE PINK. HE WAS HAVING THE dream again. Perhaps, this time, the thousand suckers—some the size of a pinhead, some a pot lid—finally worked open the flesh of his thighs. This time, they made their way inside. He wrapped his arms around the body, saw himself from a remove, from above, couldn't tell if this was an act of fighting, or love.

ONE TUESDAY, IN 1874, REVEREND MOSES HARvey woke up cold in his house at 3 Devon Row, sweating, the fingernails of his left hand raking the wall which was thinly papered with anchors emblazoned on faux lace. Sleep-dazed, he reached for his sternum with his chin. The lowermost whiskers of his gray beard reached the concave spoon of flesh and he scratched himself by shaking his head *No.* His wife, Sarah, watched him from her own bed on the other side of the small room, the drool cooling on her cheek, the icy Newfoundland sea air creeping in through the walls. She watched him as he clung to the wallpaper as if pulling himself from a mine on a rope of knotted scarves, watched him as he muttered, in Gaelic, a language which she imperfectly understood, *máthair, máthair*, which she knew meant *mother*, then *máthair SHÚIGH, máthair SHÚIGH,* which she translated as *sea arrow*, a nickname she knew, due to her husband's piety as a naturalist and sea-monster obsessive, that the Old Irish lent to the majesty of the squid, then *ollmhór… máthair shúigh ollmhór.* Sarah was unsure about this last word.

In their dining room, the Victorian cherrywood table lay dormant under three purple doilies. The gold-framed oil of an abandoned, beached sailboat clung to its nail. The hutch with pewter latches that they brought with them to Newfoundland in pieces and then reassembled held two Bibles, shards of a broken hand mirror, and twelve linen napkins, each with unique stains that would never come out. The huntboard pie safe held in its drawers a scattering of fishing hooks and bobbers, snarls of line, brass "birdcage" reels and stop-latch reels with heart-shaped screws and, Harvey's favorite, a silver reel with a rim pull-stop, hard rubber handle, and knurled counterbalance knob, and a “reverse-S” handle that Harvey felt was blatantly diaphanous.

The earliest of ocean lights crept into their bedroom, and Sarah stared beyond her hay mattress to the stone floor, littered with her husband’s blue rubber slippers (perfect for dry land, he would say, and perfect for the sea). Some days, he would deliver a sermon to his congregants in these slippers, before leaving the church for a devout walk along the shore. She reached to her driftwood nightstand and pulled a hairpin from its tomato-shaped cushion. Before she could slide it into her hair, Moses sat up straight in his bed and said, “I had it again, Sarah. I almost had it.”

“The squid,” she said, and sucked at her fingers, which tasted of last night’s rum plums. She fashioned her dark hair into three loops and secured it with the pin. The ivory handle felt good in her right hand—worn like her mother’s cheek. Her mother whom they left to die alone in Ireland.

“This time,” Moses said, his voice sounding so old to her this morning, like ripping paper, “it was huge. It was *giant*.”

Sarah closed her eyes and thought of Belfast, then Maryport, England. Both were cold, but not as cold as Newfoundland. Both were gray, but not as gray as Newfoundland. They came here October 4, 1852, and Moses, then thirty-two years old, began serving St. Andrew's Free Church. Sarah began staring out to sea. A giant holding smaller giants.

~

NO ONE CAN TELL ME WHERE TO FIND IT. NOT the young policeman chatting up the pretty jogger in yellow butt-hugger shorts on Water Street (*Devon Row? Moses Harvey? Squid? Are you sure you're talkin' about St. John's,* New*foundland?*). Not the docent at The Rooms, the "new" Newfoundland Museum, built with some misappropriated stainless-steel-and-glass ultramodern dedication to some anorexic hip-bone angularism, which looks like the offspring of the phoenix and crapola. The docent hadn't even heard–*ever*–of the giant squid, or of Harvey, or Devon Row.

Not the androgynous waitress at Bacalao restaurant, up the hill from The Narrows, the ocean foaming at the mouth against the rocks, the boathouses decorated with plumeria, the clapboard twine shops, the fishing stages with the concrete floors stained purple with old guts, the multicolored rowhouses, the crushed dog sleds at the curbs, the bars hazing tourists with shots of the awful Screech rum and the customary postswallow lip-kissing of the dead raw cod, the forts and cannons, bodies of water with names like Quidi Vidi and Deadman, where

I ate a blur of a lunch, shards of cod tongue with green peppercorn aioli, caribou roulade with juniper, seal flipper pie, lobster omelet, sweetbread with partridgeberry and bakeapple jams, Lady of the Woods birch-sap wine (*Devon Row? I've never heard of it. No one I know has ever spoke of it. But I can tell you that the roads outside St. John's—the ones into the interior? They're the worst they've been in years, my stepson says. He just came back from gathering wood there. You see all those broken dog sleds . . . ?*).

At the neighboring table, two old women in the precise lace kerchiefs and black-framed glasses and billowing silk neck-scarves and mauve lady sportcoats that scream *Historical Society* take down the last of their shared crème brûlée. Long-finished, digesting, I wait for the ladies to pay up, then stalk them out the rear door of the restaurant, startling them in the blinding sun of the parking lot with an anxious *Pardon me, ladies!* The one with the horse dentures does the talking, the other, the slightly built one, rifling through her baby blue clamshell handbag. From inside the bag snakes a stench not like the one that snaked from many of my Grandma Ruth's flea-market purses—clove, orange peel, camphor—but a decidedly Newfoundland brew of fish eyes and astringent berry and salt.

She holds her huge breasts aloft with her crossed forearms and says, like an Irish Julia Child, "My sister especially was outraged that St. John's wasn't interested in preserving their historical buildings, and I thought, you know, outrage is a good idea."

The silent, but apparently outraged, sister dabs at her lips with her lime scarf. Her hands shaking, she retrieves three old credit card receipts from her rank purse, and tears the proprietary addresses from their tops. She hands the scraps to the larger one.

"Oh, yes," she says, "try these places. Probable locations, they are. This one"–gripping and shaking in my face a meager scrap of receipt as if strangling a hummingbird–"first."

The women wish me luck, totter toward their tiny car. The address is for Devon House over on Duckworth Street. *Could this be the old Harvey place?* I finger the map in my pocket, walk from parking lot to street. Stuffed full, I crave something comforting, and look out for an ice-cream parlor. Rumor has it that there is one in town that keeps their flavors cold with blocks of glacial icebergs.

Down the hill, the ocean roars. In it, the overfished cod desperately try to propagate their species.

ᔓ

I FIND NO ICE-CREAM PARLOR. I TRY TO TAKE comfort in history, or at least, in brochures:

The first ice-cream parlor in North America was opened by colonist and confectioner Philip Lenzi in New York City in 1776. We didn't wait very long after Independence to pursue our cold-craving sweet-teeth and then-distant cultural obesity problem.

> As for America . . . ice cream is recorded to have been served as early as 1744 (by the lady of Governor Blandon of Maryland, nee Barbara Jannsen, daughter of Lord Baltimore), but it does not appear to have been generally adopted until much later in the century. Although its adoption then owed much to French contacts in the period following the American Revolution, Americans shared 18th century England's tastes and the English preference for ice creams over water ices, and proceeded enthusiastically to make ice cream a national dish. (*Oxford Companion to Food*, Alan Davidson [Oxford: Oxford University Press, 1999], pp. 392–93).

Ice cream lover George Calvert, first of a line of Lord Baltimores, established colonies in both Maryland (obviously) and Newfoundland, including Ferryland (formerly Colony of Avalon), where, in 1935, resident Joe Ezekiel caught, and took a blurry photo with, a giant squid.

Oddly enough, blogger Steven King (not Stephen), in his October 22, 2010, post titled, "The Story of the Emerald Dragon," named his giant-squid-expert character George Calvert. In King's piece, Calvert is being interviewed on the radio, an interview which includes the following Q & A: "[Interviewer:] Now George, we talk about how big the giant squid is, and an animal of that size can be dangerous, right? [George Calvert:] Oh, sure."

From the article, "Mysterious Monster from the Deep," by John Dyson, originally published in *Reader's Digest*:

> Seldom has a giant squid been taken alive, but a 20 year old Newfoundland fisherman achieved that on a crisp fall morning in 1935. The monster's appearance . . . , in Conception Bay, meant only one thing to young Joe Ezekiel–a mountain of bait and dog food. The [squid's] crimson arms and tentacles gave it the look of an immense flower as

Ezekiel rowed his dory straight for it. He gave the boat a last hard thrust... hurled his 11-kilogram anchor....

Serpent-like... tentacles longer than the five metre dory coiled in oozing knots and their convulsion made waves.... Ezekiel heaved in the anchor rope and snubbed the boat up to the monster's huge tapered body. One tentacle, thick as a stovepipe and studded with suckers, writhed above the surface. Ezekiel grabbed it. The creature, perhaps sick, seemed... listless as Ezekiel threw a couple of half hitches around the tentacle with a rope.

But he kept his fish knife handy..., as laboriously he towed the monster into shore. Jetting clouds of a musky ink, it turned the surface of the cove black. Twenty men who had seen Ezekiel's brave capture from their harborside windows hauled it up the shingle beach. As the squid died, its brilliant red color turning a mottled blue, then a milky white, they paced out its length–8.5 metres.

Ezekiel shrouded his monster in a tarpaulin. News of the capture spread rapidly, and carloads of sightseers came.... Joe charged ten cents a look and in two days made $30.00.... [H]e sold the squid to a scientist for $10.00... stored it in the

> local fish freezer, but that night the freezer caught fire and the monster was destroyed.
>
> . . . Joe Ezekiel remains one of the few . . . to have caught . . . one of the world's most . . . terrifying creatures, more bizarre than anything appearing in Star Wars.

Most zoologists agree that the giant squid is cooler than a Lightsaber, but the jury is out on what has become known in certain cultish circles as the Yoda Comparison.

As in the details of *Moby-Dick* prior to the great expedition, descriptions of giant squid captures somehow fuse the miraculously boring with the erotic: the 11-kilogram anchor with the immense flower, the 5-metre dory with oozing knots and their convulsion, the $30.00 and the extra $10.00 with a last hard thrust and jetting clouds of black ink.

I'd like to believe that Ezekiel, surely an ice-cream lover himself, spent at least five percent of his forty-buck haul on multiple scoops of strawberry.

From "Appendix D: A Further Species of Giant Squid (Architeuthis sp.) from Newfoundland Waters" by Nancy Frost:

> The animal must have been in the last stages of exhaustion, for Jos. Ezekiel, a young fisherman, was able to drag it to the beach with the aid of a small boat . . .
>
> This organ [the common tube connecting the squid's ink sac to its rectum] was extremely fragile.

From "The Breaking of the Bread: The Development of the Eucharist According to Acts," by Eugene LaVerdiere:

> Ezekiel, when God commanded him to eat food that was unclean . . . symbolize[d] how it would be for the Israelites dispersed among the nations, "Oh no, Lord God! . . . never has any unclean meat entered my mouth" (Ezekiel 4:14) . . . The Christians, therefore, like the Jews, avoided many foods eaten by the Gentiles who had no such kosher laws . . . Clams, for example, lobster and squid are unclean . . . for the early Christians and Jews, since they had neither fins nor scales. . . . Gentiles . . . ridiculed Jews for not eating it.

From "Ezekiel: God's Prophet and His Puzzling Book," by Preston A. Taylor:

The word "likeness" in Ezekiel chapter 1 is used fourteen times to give an idea of what he saw, and "like" is used six times, and the word "appearance" is used twenty-eight times. The words "lightning" and "lamps" are used one time each (1:13). The prophet uses poetic language and word pictures to describe what he saw. What he saw was a vision, but there was reality behind the image. The Bible says, "No man can see God and live" (Exodus 33:20). Thus, the revelation of God comes in a semblance, likeness, or appearance. We're on a better road to understanding Ezekiel when we don't take him too literally. The truth is there, but the truth is in symbols.

Take an example of an image or likeness of something. The term "ice cream" brings a lot of ideas to one's mind. Some may see an ice cream freezer, a big bowl of ice cream, or an ice cream cone. Ezekiel saw something "like a lamp" that was darting back and forth within the fire and cloud. Visions. Hmm!

~

IN 1998, LLOYD HOLLETT, FORMERLY OF THE NEWfoundland Provincial Department of Forestry, opened, in an old dairy barn that resembles a barracks, the Newfoundland Insectarium. He had a vision. In it is the display of Hollett's enviable collection of insects and other arthropods, which, depending, delights and revolts cadres of field-tripping schoolchildren from the province. The Insectarium contains three levels of "mounted and live displays," the latter of which include butterflies, stick insects, tarantulas, scorpions, giant cockroaches, a leaf-cutter ant colony, and honeybees in a glass "hive." Depending on the variety, and on the constitution of the visitor, paying customers are offered the opportunity to touch, and even hold, the insects. Hollett's personal favorites are the arthropods, which are invertebrates with an exoskeleton, jointed appendages, and segmented body. They are a diverse group and include among their members caterpillars, scorpions, spider crabs, and giant squid (which is really a cephalopod–a classification which derives from the Greek for *head foot,* a beast whose feet sprout from its head–or, as Hollett calls it, "the arthropod of the sea").

Hollett stands quietly, hands on his hips, watching his patrons watch his insects. His beard is one of those too-neat beards, as if he shaves with a protractor. He is soft-spoken, soft-bellied, the poster boy for the Sensitive Male. His shirt is purple and faux-Polo. The two white buttons are buttoned. He resembles more of a meerkat or mole or mole rat or honey badger or fruit bat than an insect. Maybe a caterpillar. Hollett walks me around, telling me about leafcutter ants and beehives and spiders and butterflies, before stopping to observe some of his younger guests.

An older kid tries to hold back the rush of urine so he doesn't embarrass himself before his friends while holding an emperor scorpion, forcing the most tortured smile I've ever seen.

The interior of the Insectarium recalls an unfinished barn, the skeletal structure visible—a disturbingly high ceiling, lots of nice smooth-polished wood beams and rafters, eye-level glass cases, and a blue-green tile floor that evokes river tributaries. The place is all swallow and gape, all log cabin and humongous rib cage, and indeed, the visitor feels like a bit of food, moving along the fluttering tract of some giant ocean beast, gawking at the smaller, still-living things it previously ingested.

In addition to the live displays, the Insectarium includes mounted displays of bugs from six geographical world zones (Australian Zone, Afrotropical Zone, Indo-Malayan Zone, et al.), a special local section on Newfoundland crawlies, picnic tables, a koi pond, a gift shop, and an ice-cream parlor.

~

PREPARING THE GHOST

I STARTED THINKING A LOT ABOUT THE GIANT squid in 1995. It had something to do with the weather. I drove an ice-cream truck along the streets of suburban Chicago during the awful and now-renowned summer heat wave that killed nearly 800 people over the course of five days. The ice-cream truck was an old, rickety converted mail truck. It was doorless on both sides, open to the weather. A hole had long ago rusted through the truck's bottom, through which the exhaust would seep.

Beneath this hot midwestern air mass–heat indices over 120 degrees Fahrenheit, humidity ballistic–within which many small children, and old, impoverished, living-alone adults succumbed to death (according to the *Encyclopedia of Chicago*, "Over 70 percent of the victims were aged 65 and above; and African American mortality rates were roughly 1.5 times higher than those for whites. The heat wave deaths were concentrated in the predominantly African American community areas on the South and West Sides of Chicago, the places that also have high mortality rates and low life expectancy during normal times. The extreme weather helped to make visible some of the new dangers related to aging, isolation, and concentrated poverty in Chicago."), making the heat wave the deadliest environmental event in Chicago history, I tooled around in that awful ice-cream truck, thinking of anything cooler, in a giant sort of way–the kind of cool that can envelop a person, the kind of meditation that would allow me to live through the heat of the truck and the attendant exhaust.

I thought of the ocean. Of the giants therein. I thought of my grandfather—Poppa Dave—dead since 1986 and obese since he was a toddler—swimming with said giants in the numbingly cold depths of some watery afterlife. Perhaps I even thought of aging and isolation. Perhaps I noticed how some neighborhoods in Chicago were poorer than others; how ice-cream purchases reflected demographics; how, in some neighborhoods—the apartment-heavy ones, the ones where folks congregated around the single public pool—the awful, sticky-sweet, frozen bubble gum ball (which shattered in the mouth like glass when crushed with the molars) ice cream bars—your Screwballs and Bubble Plays, your Free Kicks and Shoot Hoops (odd how these synthetic bars, saturated with dye and without any discernible flavor besides *Sweet*, often adopted sports themes)—would constitute most of the sales, and how in others, on the richer side of the tracks, the cookie-cutter homes and aluminum siding and (at least) two-car garages and private above- or in-ground swimming pools, and vanity license plates boasting patriarchal professions, I would quickly sell out of the premium bars—the Lipton Iced Tea bars and high-fat Häagen-Dazs singles (some of which had macadamia nuts in them).

I tuned out the repetitive tinkling of "The Entertainer" and sold a shitload of ice cream. I gained quite a bit of weight that summer, on a twelve-Sno-Cone-and-six-Choco-Taco-a-day fix just to keep cool and nourished. I had long hair down to my ass and wore a beige beret and smoked a shitload of marijuana and ate my weight in crappy Good Humor ice cream and thought about squid and my grandfather. I was often told that I resembled the stoner character of Slater (played by Rory Cochrane) in Richard Linklater's *Dazed and Confused* (1993), and I tried, repeatedly and unsuccessfully, to use such a physical affiliation to woo suburban girls one or two years younger than me (whose fathers, I could tell from their license plates were ATTRNY 1's or SURGN 66's), who would often run from backyard lawns in their bathing suits, crimped hair wet and squidy from an afternoon of weathering the heat on sprinkler-fueled Slip'N Slides, and Wet Bananas, and Crocodile Miles, tentacular, all.

ᘓ

ONE TUESDAY IN 1916, MY POPPA DAVE WAS BORN. Moses Harvey had been dead fifteen years, and my Poppa Dave, from the date of his birth to the date of his death in 1986, never heard of him. But Poppa Dave was no stranger to giant things. He was born prematurely, *a real strand of spaghetti,* my Grandma Ruth, his wife, would say when retelling the story post-'86, of her late husband's birth, *a real little nothing.*

Poppa Dave's mother, Dorothy—a Polish expat who boated into New York City while pregnant, who watched her husband, Milton, rename the family upon stepping onto American soil when the immigration official, a blond Irish boy with beet-red cheeks and a broken lower lip, couldn't understand the thickly Yiddish-accented pronunciation of *Falushnik*, forcing Milton, in his famous short-tempered frustration, to take the name of the man in front of him, *Frank*—birthed her only child in a one-room Brooklyn tenement a stone's throw from Coney Island.

Worried about his tiny, premature size, and worried about what the doctor said—the doctor, sad-eyed, carrying his green leather medical case in a hand that had just begun to shake without conscious provocation, who made house calls to all the freshly immigrated folks in that Brooklyn tenement—about how malnourished this baby was—still a fetus, really, cruelly extracted too early from the womb—about how this baby would surely die in the thin blue blankets laid in the corner of that Brooklyn tenement, Dorothy began, as her poor, turn-of-the-century east European Jewish mother blood dictated, to overfeed this premature wailing thing that was soon to balloon into my lifelong obese, operatically diabetic grandfather.

Great-Grandma Dorothy, who had long been six feet

under, and maybe a little deeper even, by the time I was born, force-fed Poppa Dave so neurotically, and from such an early age, that this act, initially intended to secure his place among the living postpremature birth, was the primary agent of his premature death. She would wake him, as a child, at various intervals during the night—midnight, 2:30 A.M., 4:30 A.M.—in order to stuff his half-asleep face with boiled potatoes and schmaltz—rendered chicken fat that she mixed with salt and a little paprika—slathered over white bread.

I imagine Poppa Dave, a small boy, watching his mother's middle-of-the-night silhouette fill the doorway, the holy horror of silver spoon ringing the lip of a dish, the reek of fat and tuber. Dread is . . .

Though he was obese at age four, Dorothy continued this practice, believing she was doing the right thing—keeping her boy healthy and alive with lipids—until Poppa Dave was drafted by the U.S. Army to serve in World War II. Miraculously, in spite of his size (he was 5 feet 3 inches tall, but round as a medicine ball) and flat feet, he passed the what-I-expect-were-fairly-lenient-and-perhaps-even-desperate physical fitness tests, and was gifted with uniform and weapon.

Poppa Dave told me, a year before his death, that he developed his love of music while trying to sing himself back to sleep after Dorothy's OCD-fueled night feedings. That he later became a musician—a saxophonist in a big Dixieland-style jazz band—and played the Borscht Belt, the Catskill Mountain resort circuit in Upstate New York, was something to which his mother, who died prematurely herself of all the typical things that killed off motherly Polish-Jewish expats living in Brooklyn tenements a stone's throw from Coney Island, was never to bear witness—this artistic side effect to her forced after-hours gorge-fests.

I wonder what songs Poppa Dave would sing to himself, reaching again for sleep with a greasy throat, and all the blood in his belly. In 1916, the year of his birth, the most popular songs included:

All Heaven Is Calling Mavourneen (Geoffrey O'Hara, music; Katherine Ward, lyrics)
The Chicken Walk (Irving Berlin)
Ireland Must Be Heaven, for My Mother Came from There (Fred Fisher, music; Joe McCarthy, Howard Johnson, lyrics)
Mammy's Little Coal Black Rose (Richard A. Whiting, music; Raymond Egan, lyrics)
My Mother's Rosary
Oh, How She Could Yacki Hacki Wicki Wacki Woo (Albert Von Tilzer, music; Stanley Murphy, Charles McCarron, lyrics)

There's a Quaker Down in Quaker Town (Alfred Solman, music; David Berg, lyrics)

Wake Up, America! (Jack Glogau, music; George Graff, lyrics)

Where Did Robinson Crusoe Go with Friday on Saturday Night? (George W. Meyer, music; Sam M. Lewis, Joe Young, lyrics)

Yaaka Hula Hickey Dula (Pete Wendling, music; E. Ray Goetz, Joe Young, lyrics)

The top ten songs of 1986, the year of Poppa Dave's death, were:

1. "That's What Friends Are For" (Dionne & Friends)
2. "Walk Like an Egyptian" (Bangles)
3. "On My Own" (Patti Labelle & Michael McDonald)
4. "The Way It Is" (Bruce Hornsby & The Range)
5. "You Give Love a Bad Name" (Bon Jovi)
6. "Greatest Love of All" (Whitney Houston)
7. "There'll Be Sad Songs" (Billy Ocean)
8. "How Will I Know" (Whitney Houston)
9. "Kyrie" (Mr. Mister)
10. "Kiss" (Prince & The Revolution)

Somewhere in between, chronologically and thematically, along the continuum stretching from Wendling,

Goetz, and Young's "Yaaka Hula Hickey Dula" to Bon Jovi's "You Give Love a Bad Name," Poppa Dave wrote his own most popular song, never recorded, but a Borscht Belt staple. The song reflected a dream he often had as an overfull child perpetually digesting, of some indistinct multilimbed angel twisting in the depths of some unnamable sea, as he, Poppa Dave (then just Dave) swam toward the creature and saved its life. (I remember Poppa Dave, a fat man, being an expert floater in a long line of public pools stretching from Illinois [where we lived] to Florida [where Poppa Dave and Grandma Ruth retired to a planned community complex with "Phase II" in its title], wherein he would lie on his back on the water's surface, hand behind his head, the other anchoring a book to his soft sternum, floating and reading, floating and reading.)

Like many songwriters in those days, he turned his dream-narrative into a new "dance" which never, ever, came even close to being a "craze." Poppa Dave told me, a year before his death, that he thought the angel was a squid, and his song was thus called "Squid Jump."

The attendant dance, which he himself concocted, perhaps also in sleep, involved Step One: facing your partner and waving your arms in a squidlike fashion up and down, then Step Two: jumping into the air, doing a half-turn (so you and your partner are now back-to-back) and performing the same squiddy move, then Step Three: another jumping half-turn (which, honestly, I cannot picture Poppa Dave doing out of water), re-facing your partner, and repeating the whole thing (Steps 1–3). The song, while predominantly instrumental, involved a bridge (driven by the drums) that included three lines of lyrics. These lines were (1) *Do the Squid Jump!* (2) *Jump up!* and (3) *Wave your arms like this!*

Poppa Dave, long dead now, lives for me in part in these three imperatives in search of craze, and communion.

~

I DON'T KNOW IF MOSES HARVEY WOKE UP COLD and sweating. I do know that he took the first photograph ever of a giant squid, but I don't know if it was on a Tuesday. Maybe his fingernails never scratched at his wallpaper, and maybe his wallpaper never bore lacy anchor designs. I know nothing of his wife Sarah's sleep drool, or of the draftiness of their Newfoundland home. I know much of Harvey's marine obsessions, but little of how said obsessions manifested in his dreams. I don't know if the Harveys stuffed their mattress with hay for additional softness, or if oceanic detritus littered the stone floor of their bedroom. I don't even know if their floor was stone. I know nothing of Harvey's preferred footwear, or of the materials that composed their probable nightstands, or of the cushions that housed, or didn't house, Sarah's hairpins. Who knows what Moses and Sarah said to each other upon waking, or what their fingers smelled of, or what Sarah's mother's cheek felt like? I am mythmaking, I suppose.

I know a lot about shitty ice cream, but so little of Poppa Dave's childhood. I have no picture of my great-grandmother Dorothy, or her husband Milton, or their first tenement in Brooklyn. I'm not even sure if it was only a single room. I don't know about the doctor who wrongfully predicted Poppa Dave's infant death, or the color of his medical case, or the color of the blankets in which my baby grandfather was diagnosed to die.

ᔓ

"THERE'S ALWAYS ROOM FOR ICE CREAM"–PERHAPS the sequence of words that Poppa Dave uttered most frequently, at least during the time our lives overlapped, 1976 to 1986, when I was within earshot, next to "Goddamn it to hell, Ruth!" which he hurled hourly at my grandmother whenever she complained about the cigar ash that he was dropping ever deeper into the awful peach shag of her carpeting. I never saw Poppa Dave finish a meal without moving on to ice cream. And I never saw Poppa Dave finish his ice cream without moving on to a cigar.

~

LLOYD HOLLETT SAYS, "THE INITIAL IDEA TO have an Ice Cream Parlor at the [Newfoundland] Insectarium was to help with the generation of revenue. We are a private business that survives without any subsidies from government. We get twenty thousand visitors each season (May to October) so any extra money we can generate is important. Having said this, we have found that the Ice Cream does not generate much revenue but our visitors really enjoy it. We therefore decided to keep it more as a treat for our visitors than anything else. Besides, after you spend a while in a warm greenhouse (our butterfly pavilion) with 1000 tropical butterflies, it is nice to be able to have a nice cold ice cream.

"Ice cream and insects are not an odd mix if you look at insects and ice cream together–they are both beautiful things and both are joys of this life!

"[We have] no special [ice-cream] flavors that are insect themed. We thought about topping them with chocolate-coated crickets but felt it would turn off too many people! We . . . feature 10 flavors including Death By Chocolate, Turtle Tracks and Bubblegum."

In *nice* and in *beautiful things* and in *joys of this life!* Lloyd Hollett, as we all do, is simplifying unnamable obsession into the sort of meaning that is easily transferable. He's mailing an envelope to us. In it is a soft, folded piece of paper with writing on it–the acceptable mask for the twitching fairy dust that allows him to fly. And we read the letter and we nod as if we understand. We nod, as if *sincerely* means what it says.

ᔓ

THE DEATH OF POPPA DAVE, THE DEATH OF THE Giant Squid, the Death of Moses Harvey, the Death of so many Chicagoans in 1995. Death by Ice Cream. Death by Diabetes. Death by Heatwave. Death by Giant Squid. Death by Chocolate sounds right. Death by Scorpion sounds right. Death by Butterfly doesn't. Death by Bubblegum doesn't.

Our obsessions allow us to live, then take us away. We make myths of them. Grandfathers. Squid. Insects. Ice Cream. We mythologize the actual, just because it's unusual. See: *the mythical giant squid*, which isn't mythical at all–it's been photographed and captured (dead), it's been encased in Plexiglas in the Smithsonian's National Museum of Natural History (in a room bordering that which houses the profoundly boring Hope Diamond), stretched out to its maximum length in its thermoplastic coffin–unimpressive, dead, anorexic, a behemoth snot hanging horizontally, its poor legs limp, spaghettical.

I'm not sure which is worse: death by myth or death of myth. I'm not sure how to turn that previous sentence, or sentiment, into an ice-cream flavor.

ᘏ

I ADMIT IT: I MYTHOLOGIZED LLOYD HOLLETT. I asked him about his other obsessions besides insects and ice cream. Luckily, for the purposes of this essay, he said, "I have always been intrigued by the giant squid. My wife's uncle actually found one washed up on a local beach when he was a teenager. It was collected later by Memorial University. It is so interesting that such a large creature can live on this planet and virtually nothing is known about its habits, food, and life in general.

"Nature has shaped my life from an early age, when I spent most of my time outside, exploring the countryside. I would spend countless hours combing local beaches looking for all kinds of flotsam and jetsam. Most exciting thing ever found was a marine flare that had washed ashore. After setting it off one night in our quiet fishing village we had the whole community in an uproar. Luckily nobody ever found out who did it!!!"

I wonder if that flare was flotsam or jetsam. I think about the unique rubric each of us uses to determine which from which.

I imagined Hollett clad in bright orange superhero

hip-waders and thick glasses–a sort of outdoorsy, but still wonderfully geeky, Thor. Hopeful, excited, I asked him what his favorite movie was. I question my own rubric.

He said, "*Christmas Vacation*."

~

FOLKS WHO ATTEMPT TO RECONSTRUCT DINOsaur bones and/or design the Neanderthalic dioramas for the National Museum of Natural History speak of the professional leeway they're allowed to fill in the historic geological time gaps, the blanks, the missing pieces of both actual, physical reconstruction and the narrative leashed to the reconstruction. They admit that much of their process is speculatory, and this is accepted as an unavoidable norm within the field. They admit that life *science* is an inexact science.

~

MEMORY IS A TANTRUM.

~

TITLE OF AN ARTICLE MOSES HARVEY WROTE IN 1864: "Human Progress–Is it Real?"

~

IF ONE WERE TO SPLIT A SERIES OF HUMAN BEINGS in half lengthwise, one would find, as according to the responsible gene sequence, that our hearts would, more often than not, tip toward the left of us. Of course, there are mutants among us. Mutants whose involuntary penchants for recessivity deem that *their* (it's not *our* anymore) hearts tip toward the right side. Linguistically, these right-hearted folks, though in the minority, are more "correct" than the rest of us—*right* (and the word *dexterous*) derives from the Latin *dexter.* Folks who favored their right sides (right-handed people, for instance) were seen as dexterous people. Folks who favored their left sides were seen as evil, in cahoots with the devil; left-handedness was seen as a sign of bastardy, and such mutants were often forced to unnaturally favor their right hands. *Left* derives from the Latin word *sinister.* This, linguistically, is what our hearts are. As human beings invented this language, this is how we see ourselves.

Countless variations that deviate from the dominant version are capable of arising in the same singular species. These "right-hearted" people are mutant truths. Recessive ones. Somewhere, in the recesses of these recessive versions of our dominant truths, behind a daisy chain of lanterns and Darwin's theories drunk and conga-lining, Rudolph Valentino was a blond.

൱

SO: PERHAPS DOROTHY WAS BEAUTIFUL. MAYBE Poppa Dave never resembled spaghetti. Perhaps Hollett deserves to be mythologized in spite of being "a big fan of John Candy." I'd like to believe that Moses Harvey did wake that morning in 1874 with cold hands. That Sarah woke with peas of sweat on her tiny Adam's apple. That Moses prayed and ate a breakfast of cinnamon bread. Perhaps he strolled the beach and smelled the giant before he saw it—all-encompassing, overstuffing his nostrils, Great-Grandma Dorothy shoveling the marine but vaguely deciduous scent of the mythical squid up his nose as if it were schmaltz into my Poppa. Perhaps, upon seeing it, Harvey, though not even close to fluent in Yiddish, Dorothy's primary language, *plotzed.* Maybe he succumbed to awe—faced with myth made actual—to craze and communion and an odd feeling of Irish homesickness. Maybe he wrote the first draft of his next sermon right there, in front of the beast, washed up into Newfoundland, its old land lost, its deep ocean misplaced, as the sunrise scored the sky with slashes of pink. Perhaps the thought of transporting this squid to his home, and suspending it over his bathtub, didn't occur to him until later.

൱

The giant squid as silk lampshade.
The giant squid as a lampshade made of silkworms,
trapped with staples, but still wildly spinning.
The giant squid as the pet silkworms to whom my wife
fed beet greens, so they would spin red.
The giant squid as metaphor.
The giant squid as dominant metaphor begetting a
recessive one.
The giant squid as Alyssa Milano.
The giant squid as teenage crushes.
The giant squid as my parents' house.
The giant squid as watching TV with my parents.
The giant squid as octopus.
The giant squid as guppy.
The giant squid as Ruthie, my sister's pet goldfish
circa 1981, so named after my grandmother due to
a red spot on its forehead.
The giant squid as a flushing toilet taking a body
away.
The giant squid as appetizer.
The giant squid as a six-year-old muttering *Fuck you-
ton, Isaac Newton* at the bus stop after failing his
science test.
The giant squid as Dawn Seckler kissing me in the
Adlai E. Stevenson High School parking lot after

graduation, forever erasing the tether between my own personal gravity and the public earth.

The giant squid as being careful.

The giant squid as the stingless bees the size of basmati rice grains in the Cardamom Hills of Kerala, India, which produce a black medicinal honey that can cure most types of blindness.

The giant squid as first kiss as gravity as tiny bees without stingers as things that should hurt us, but don't.

The giant squid as premature birth and premature death.

The giant squid as way too logical.

The giant squid as notes scrawled on a barf bag.

The giant squid as Möbius strip.

The giant squid as ______________ forced through a ______________ by a ______________ with a ______________ and the mounted marlin stuffed with love letters, some sixty years old.

The giant squid as all the items in my dead grandmother's house:

mothballs
salmon patties
red breakfast nook
illicit Froot Loops
squishy Vitamin E pills exploding on a silver-

painted bedroom doorframe because I squeezed
them too hard
pictures of us
The giant squid as my father.
The giant squid as my father's beard, as my father's
father, as my father's father's
saxophone
arteries
diabetes
credos
bad jokes in Yiddish
bad fingers on a baby piano
The giant squid as family tree.
The giant squid as sapling, sap.
The giant squid as an excuse to say *giant.*
The giant squid as an excuse not to say *grand.*

~

ST. ANDREW, FOR WHOM MOSES HARVEY'S NEWfoundland church was named, was crucified not by nails but by rope on a saltire, or X-shaped cross, in the city of Patras, Greece, the sole city in Greece that I have seen, and the city in Greece that I have seen engulfed in the flames of a wildfire, in which I ate a street gyro stuffed with awful French fries, and the city I couldn't afford to leave after the railway system went on strike, and the city in which the local police turned their dogs loose on me, mistakenly believing that I was the American drug smuggler that they'd been hunting for weeks, and the city in Greece that ruined Greece for me and drove me, when the boats back to Italy started running again, on a beeline to Narvik, Norway, the end of the rail line, and beyond, where I cast the last of my drachmas into the Arctic Ocean, and the same city that Grandma Ruth and Poppa Dave visited decades earlier where Poppa Dave, at an outdoor cafe table, penned his instrumental jazz tune *The Wandering Jew* on a cocktail napkin, a song which I never heard him play on the saxophone (for which it was written)–just the piano, one time on the piano, as I sat next to him on the bench in New York, Ruthie chastising him for the solemnity of it, and Poppa Dave downturning his eyes after the last notes, releasing his fat foot from the pedals which squeaked and dampened in the hollow of the wood, and silently and with trembling hands, rubbing my back as Ruthie flipped salmon patties and told my *shayna madela* sister that she had a *punim* to drive the boys crazy.

Though Andrew was once thought to be a common Jewish name, there is no record of any Hebrew or Aramaic name for this saint.

∾

I FOLLOW THE TWO OLD HISTORICAL SOCIETY ladies' directions along the steep alleys of St. John's to Duckworth Street. Devon House is an art gallery taking up three floors of a historic home—lots of crown molding and wicker baskets and sachets of potpourri, the exterior brick adorned with brightly painted papier-mâchè starfish with glued-on, oddly sentient, eyes. Stained-glass vases etched with fish, carved stairwell banisters thicker than me, old charcoal carpet making love to mildew. Blue arrows on the wall: MORE TO SEE UPSTAIRS! And up the groaning stairs, more paintings of fish and flowers, beautiful young St. John's women, arms sleeved in tattoos, tending the hanging wolf plates, the wooden birds with oversized beaks, the landscape photos of wonderfully mundane waterfalls. And pillows sewn with fish, and quilts sewn with fish, and lampshades made of antlers, and shawls sewn with fish. Beautiful young St. John's women with pierced lips polishing the brass bells on the mantles of the old iron fireplaces, logs decoratively half-burnt in the maws, or, bricked-over, festooned with throw rugs and flower vases, paintings of birds in trees and fish in water. And for sale—only $40 apiece!—ONE OF A KIND LIMITED EDITION CERAMIC VESSELS: 40 CUPS, 40 YEARS: coffee mugs etched with fishing paraphernalia—lures and reels—and a cornucopia of sea creatures, not one of them the squid. And: lifelike clay replicas of birds' eggs in nests, pink papier-mâchè crabs hanging from the ceiling on invisible string, masked mummer dolls with Velcro'd extremities dry-humping the old balusters. And in the pantry near the bathrooms, shelves of Kirkland coffee, Lipton Cup-a-Soup. And out the bay windows, spears of fog bisecting the mountains, the waves thundering at the Narrows, the orange barge offloading its detritus. A beautiful young St. John's woman with a silver fish in her tongue tells me: 3 Devon Row, the old Harvey home, is four doors down.

ᘛ

A TUESDAY, 1874, REVEREND MOSES HARVEY stepped from 3 Devon Row, walked the stony beach in a light morning rain. A cold pins-and-needles rain. A rain with gumption. A rain that, when it touched Harvey's skin—the backs of his hands, his cheeks and forehead—drew something from him beyond warmth. A rain with tentacles. A rain with a Hebrew name. The sky's gray soon overtook those early slashes of pink. His heart began to speed, dominantly to the left of his body's center. He smelled it before he knew what it was he was smelling. His nose began, as it did from time to time, to bleed.

The previous October 26, 1873, Moses and Sarah were taking a meal of potatoes boiled with salt and laurel on the balcony of 3 Devon Row, probably shivering in the weather, the wind marine, and predicting winter. Moses may have already been thinking about writing a tourist guide to Newfoundland, and the seductive phrase "ice jewelry" occurred to him as he gummed the tubers, as a keen way to describe the island's trees in winter. The French doors creaked forward and back in the wind, and the condensed fog dripped from the mansard roof.

Though most of their neighbors had built their own homes, Moses and Sarah had not. Though most of their neighbors had their kitchens in their stone-walled basements, prepared their meals in candlelight and cobweb, mildew and shadow, Moses and Sarah did not. Regardless, their basement retained a series of cords with bells attached to their ends, each running up throughout the house, in order to summon, in even earlier times, the servants to the subterranean kitchen. The Harveys' next-door neighbor was a moonshiner, and oftentimes they received mistaken knocks on their door from hopeful strangers looking to buy jars of bay rum, which some of the Row's residents colloquially dubbed Jakie's Gin.

Devon Row was erected by the wealthy settler couple James and Hannah Martin, who came to St. John's from Devon, England in the early 1800s. Each of the Devon Row homes, built of local brick, beams, and trusses, shared the commonality of a fireplace on every floor, basement included, a testament to the local winter, which always, like some suave pomaded vampire, talked its way inside. In later years, many of these fireplaces, including Moses's and Sarah's, would be bricked over, sometimes with the early inhabitants' incompletely burned possessions sealed up inside. If chiseled away, one may find behind the brick the charred cuff of a child's blue pajama bottom, the tarnished hip-curve of a brass "birdcage" fishing reel.

Following his autumnal walks along the shore, Moses would often warm up against a fire that Sarah had prepared for him–the one in the basement with the stone mantel onto which Harvey always planned, and failed, to carve his initials; or the one on the first floor with the mantel of Italian marble which Sarah felt was smoother than the skin of a fish, and which she may have fingered, absentmindedly, as if in meditation, throughout the days, most often when she was thinking of Ireland beneath the sculpted plaster ceiling and the wooden moldings that spiraled like the shells of snails, the poor unevolved snails who, due to the twists of their bodies inside their shells, shat in their own mouths; or the fireplace with the wooden mantelpiece, or the fireplace with the iron mantelpiece, or the fireplaces meant for the servants that the Harveys never had, in the servants' quarters that the Harveys used for storage.

When Moses was out on his walks, I picture Sarah

tapping her bare feet on the multicolored stone of the threshold, losing herself in the pleasant ticking of her own flesh against imported tile, staring at this strange blue and red world through the blue-and-red-stained porch glass; or staring through the bay windows which opened onto the street, sometimes unlatching one of the peaked hooks from its gingerbread molding, letting the air of St. John's into her hair, daring, silently, the passersby to greet her, acknowledge her presence here. She would think often of her small 1852 wedding in Cockermouth, England—it was July 7, a Wednesday, and as Moses slid the simple gold band onto her finger, Thoreau told us that it was a foggy morning and the birds were singing, and that a cowbell rang, and that meadows hold medicinal value, and that we humans need to sleep with the windows open and embrace the mist, and in this mist, Sarah said yes and Moses said yes, and they kissed, and the Irish Sea roared.

She would think often of her full and former name—Sarah Anne Browne—and of all of the silver and lace gifts she had to leave behind when, only a few months after the wedding, she and Moses lit out for this godforsaken rock.

When the Harveys arrived from Europe, they were repeatedly warned that moving into a house on St. John's Devon Row was a "risky venture, risky venture, risky venture..." As they forked the crumbling flesh of the potatoes into their mouths, they stared down the not-so-distant gun barrels of Fort William, the city's primary defense installation against invasion by sea. Or invasion by *the* sea.

Like their neighbors, Moses and Sarah knew that their tenure in their adopted home was conditional. They knew that, if some band of foreign marauders—whether organized or ragtag—attacked the city, waged a war, they would immediately be evicted, packed with their neighbors into some sardine can of a refugee camp, their residence demolished, as their adopted home committed the cardinal sin of obstructing Fort William's view of the harbor, and the pathway of its cannonballs.

"Under such a constant threat," the *Atlantic Advocate* reported, "it can be readily imagined that the inhabitants of these houses never knew if they would have a home the next day or not."

In this way, Moses and Sarah, in choosing to live where they lived, were demoted, in the eyes of the city fathers, from human beings to inhabitants. As if their immigrant status wasn't enough, this housing policy confirmed their lack of permanence here, their inability to belong, as a fixture in the city, dictated by statute. Moses and Sarah were transients here, umbrella'd beneath the threat of eviction—actual or cosmic—as they crushed pieces of potato against the roofs of their mouths with their tongues. To them, St. John's would forever be noncommittal; to St. John's, they would forever be temporary.

Though their house was never decimated due to wartime invasion, a portion of Devon Row was later flattened, long after Moses and Sarah had died, to pave a three-car parking lot for the East End branch of the Bank of Montreal, which the historical society demanded be reclad in the endemic red brick.

I wonder if Sarah pressed the butter knife through the last of her potatoes. Halved it. Expected for some reason to find a horsefly inside. I wonder if Moses had already finished, and was drumming his fingers on the balcony's railing. A stagecoach, likely drawn by at least four horses, approached the property. In it was at least one, but perhaps all three, of the boatmates who had just had their first giant-squid (which they still dubbed "Devil-fish") encounter in the seas off the coast of Portugal Cove, Newfoundland.

According to the Town of Portugal Cove's Community Profile (2003), "Tommy Picco, [his father] Theophilus Picco [sometimes spelled, Picot or Piccot or Piccott, depending on the source], and Daniel Squires were out on the water when the encounter occurred."

They were floating in a three-mile-wide strait known as "The Tickle" when the three men "spotted a huge, grayish mass spread" like some awful sail "over the surface of the sea." With a boat hook, Theophilus tickled what he later referred to as a "blob." "The supposed debris immediately showed violent signs of life–and resentment." "Instantly, the mass erupted in a spray of water," "immediately came to life," as if it were previously dead, and it took the sharp tickle of these Tickle-bound men to resurrect it. Yes! It was a *kraken*! The creature of legend who lies in wait for innocent ships, dragging the vessels to the ocean floor where it undoubtedly makes a meal of the crew entire! Tentacles like pythons! That horrendous mouth!

With its "unblinking," lidless, "dinner plate" "iridescent," "furious" "green saucer" "Argus" eyes that were "terrifyingly humanlike"–an ocular description that occurred to the men only later, perhaps late at night in their beds, allowing them to speculate on why the eyes, when associated with human beings, with themselves, made them more "terrifying;" allowing them to wonder: *If we can make of the kraken the Other, we can deal with it, but if we can associate it with our own species, this may have the negative side-effect of arousing some sort of sympathy, which may open some sort of flood-gate, which may render our reaction to the sinister coming of the waters to a mere and perfect "Holy shit!"*–[the kraken] seemed to glower.

And glower it did as this kraken-cum-Devil-fish opened "out like a huge umbrella," "its great cylindrical body pulsating," and "attacked the skiff, threatening to take the men with it," enveloping them in its "livid folds." With its "parrotlike beak," "the monster crunched deeply into the dory's gunwale." Water poured into the boat. "It was only a matter of seconds before they would all go down to a watery grave [!]" The beast shook its "six gallon keg" of a head back and forth in a violent *No!* As the boat angled into the brine of the Tickle, the fishing equipment which, just this morning the men organized so neatly–the cod jiggers and handline leads, which Theophilus made himself out of sand, salt, heavy paper, and hot lead, the cod trawls and netting needles, which Theophilus carved himself from driftwood and embedded into the nets that he knitted from gleaned twine throughout the nights of the past winter, pining, maybe, for his estranged wife, the hand gaffs and fish forks, on which Theophilus attached the handles of old shovels, on

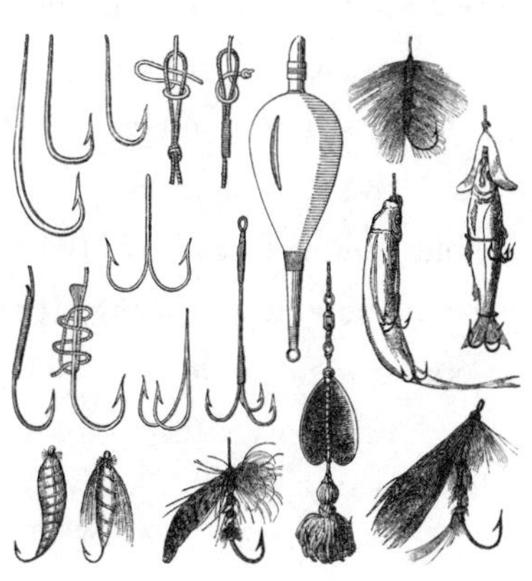

which he impaled countless fish on the sharp end made by the local St. John's blacksmith on Water Street–slid across the boat, tripping up the three men. The blade of Theo's favorite splitting knife, the one in which he carved a nude woman into the handle, sank into the top of his rubber boot. The puncheon tub overturned, littering the deck with salted fillets of cod, which somehow, in spite of their aroma, drew no flies. The cast net tumbled over on itself like some dumpy child rolling downhill, the cast net balls taking Daniel Squires out at the shins, the hauling rope coiling like a live snake around his wrists. The cast-iron bark pot, in which Theo just yesterday "barked" the nets on the beach–a procedure that involved boiling the nets in a spruce bud solution as a preservative measure–rolled toward them like some three-legged bowling ball, which they narrowly dodged. The homemade killick anchor dug in and stayed put. There were no mussel tongs because these men fished for no mussels. There was no squid jigger because, at the time, squid such as this were unjiggable.

Twelve-year-old Tommy Picco saved the men's lives by taking up a hatchet and quickly cutting off the creature's arms, which "were surprisingly soft and split apart." "The kraken spewed gallons of black ink into the water," and, in this way, the boat was freed. The larger of the two tentacles, "the gristly, twitching remainder of their brush with death," was brought ashore and fed to the village dogs. About this, Harvey cried, "How it made my heart ache to think of the loss to science inflicted by ravenous dogs! I called to mind the mischief wrought by Sir Isaac Newton's dog Diamond [who reportedly knocked over a candle with his wagging tail, setting ablaze twenty years' worth of his master's experimental notes, though many historians believe that Newton never owned pets], but it seemed nothing to this."

The smaller tentacle, 19 feet in length–which Tommy originally wanted to convert into a rope for mooring his boat–was brought to Reverend Moses, who would later refer to the appendage as Picco's "gift."

According to Harvey, the boy's first line (which immediately hooked the good Reverend) was "Would you like to buy the horn of a big squid?"

Because Harvey was, by then, a famed local eccentric and, again according to the Community Profile, "collector of biological curiosities," having published article after zoological article in such venues as the *Halifax Citizen*, *St. John's Daily News*, the *New York Evening Post*, the *Montreal Gazette*, the *St. John's Telegraph*, and the *Temperance Journal*, often utilizing cryptic pennames such as "Delta," "Locomotive," and "Nemo," the three boaters decided to haul the nearly 20-foot-long smaller tentacle to the Harvey homestead, where Sarah, upon watching the rank-smelling stagecoach approach their outdoor table—a scene with which she was surely more than familiar—probably rolled her eyes and swallowed what would be her last bite of soft potato for the evening.

Harvey, excited that his status in the community brought him another unique specimen, listened to the equally excited boaters describe their encounter, the size of the beast, and the wherewithal of their hardy prepubescent compatriot, Tommy Picco, who, after exhibiting his courage and right-handed dexterity with a hatchet, would, from this day forward, no longer be known as Little Tommy Picco.

Indeed, later, Tommy Picco became the lionized protagonist in such locally written articles as "Tentacles of Terror" and "Devils of the Deep," and the little shit even went so far as to call the severed tentacles his "trophies," while "the older men were . . . too sickened by the encounter to be interested in the mutilated remains of the seabeast." And he went so far as to call the encounter "a lark," though "the older men had not yet recovered," and he casually brought the remains to Moses Harvey in order make a few bucks, because Tommy knew that Harvey was "crazy after all kinds of strange beasts."

At the Harvey home, heart still unable to calm, Theo,

Tommy's father, "confided [to Harvey] that he would not go through such a half-hour again for all the money in the world."

Based on Tommy's story, and the size of the tentacle before him, which he caressed as if some lace-encased lover, recalling, perhaps, his first sexual experience with his wife, who was now clearing the table of the remaining plates and disappearing into the house, humming to herself, Moses Harvey determined that, with a voice shaking with adrenaline, with a tongue smeared with potato, this squid was no fewer than 72 feet long, a determination and pronouncement that allowed The Town of Portugal Cove's Community Profile to brag, some 130 years later, that "The uniqueness of Portugal Cove with regards to Tommy Picco's 'Devil-fish' is that this was the site of the first authenticated human encounter with a giant squid." Such a proclamation of authenticity rests squarely on the shoulders of Moses Harvey.

Though this event ignited what was dubbed "kraken mania" in Newfoundland, it would take until 1874, the following year, until, debatably, "the giant squid emerged from mythology."

~

THE ENCOUNTER BETWEEN HARVEY AND THE boy Picco was further immortalized in Don Reed's young adult book, *The Kraken* (1995), after Reed took to writing following his retirement from his work as a diver at California's Marine World/Africa USA. In the book, Harvey is portrayed as a man obsessed to the point of James Bondish villainy, fingering the tip of Picco's tentacle and bellowing such exclamations as, "Ha-haaa! At last! At last!"

~

EVEN HARVEY GOT INTO THIS SORT OF EXAGgerated melodrama. About the giant squid, he writes in the *American Sportsman*, "The cold, slimy grasp paralyzes the victim with terror as the powerful red mandibles devour. The more the victim writhes, it comes in contact with more and more of the disks in succession, each of which adheres, and other arms soon encircle and drag it to the central mouth . . . This monster was a mighty ugly customer."

And, in his series, "Chronicles of Punch Bowl" (about a fictional Newfoundland village), Harvey fictionalizes the Picco story, renaming him Zek Cobbiduck (and renaming Theo, Job). Harvey tells the story from the father's (Job's) perspective. After the giant squid encounter, the story ends in bed. Job Cobbiduck has long been suffering from nightmares since his son, Zek, hacked off the tentacle of the Devil-fish. In the final paragraph, Job dreams that the squid has killed both Zek, and his wife, Mary. He wakes, muttering of Portugal Cove, before succumbing to an irreversible fear-based paralysis.

ᘓ

, CHOCOLATE-CHOCOLATE CHIP

It was later determined that Portugal Cove may, indeed, possess the highest concentration of giant squid or Devil-fish in the world, a fact that may be responsible for the residents of the town's widespread penchant for supersti-tion or belief in the supernatural, if not James Bondish villainy. The giant-squid-fueled "magic" of the area is so well established, the otherwise sober Community Profile (most of which details census information [as of 2001, the population was 5,866, with an average age of 37.3, with only 75 residents claiming to speak a language other than English], average maximum and minimum tempera-tures by month [highest: July; lowest: February], average monthly levels of precipitation [highest: October; lowest: July], information about the Town Crest [containing the colors of the provincial flag, red, white, blue, and gold, and the images of a sailing ship, two fish, five loaves of bread, a sextant, a chevron, and a horse-drawn stagecoach like the one that carried the tentacle to the Harveys'] and local points of interest [Grayman's Beard: a rock outcropping above the United Church that sports icicle "whiskers" in the winter; the Ferry Terminal: "There's something about large ships moving in and out of ports that captivates everyone, young or old."; Beachy Cove: calm waters, good for swimming, allows for views of a waterfall not visible from the road; Wildlife: whales, seals, squid, sea birds, "the cry of a lone loon on a pond," "the odd lynx."]), also feels compelled to mention that:

> The area could boast that several people could cure pain caused by a toothache. These people were commonly known as charmers. There was also another person who could "cure" or stop bleeding.

> Goat Cove, an area located between Portugal Cove and St. Philip's, was known by locals as being haunted with ghosts, headless horsemen, and ferries [*sic*]. Although elderly people in the communities claim that their parents and grandparents invented the ghosts to keep the boys of St. Philip's away from the girls of Portugal Cove, the devil had apparently made an appearance near the Goat Cove Bridge. As the story goes, a Portugal Cove man was in Broad Cove drinking with friends, when on his way home he replied that he was so tired that he'd let the devil himself carry him home. Next thing the man new [*sic*], the devil was standing in front of him. The

man was so surprised that he wished the devil away. The devil left in a rage and kicked a rock along the way; leaving his hoof print in the rock.

Stories of fairies are common among Newfoundland shores. One such story from this Town is that of a "fairy baby." This baby was taken while his mother was out hanging clothes. The baby was returned a week later, but was bruised, had twigs protruding from its mouth, and the head had tripled in size. The curse cast by the fairies on the baby could not be lifted and the baby died after 3 months. Many people in the cove still know the family name of the fairy baby.

People throughout Newfoundland observe many Signs of death, such as dreaming of a wedding, a clock that hasn't worked for years suddenly beginning to tick, or window blinds falling for no apparent reason. One sign though is particular to Portugal Cove. It is said that if the Church bell rings once for no apparent reason, death or tragedy was about to occur. This was shown on the morning of November 10, 1940 when early that morning the St. Lawrence Church bell rang out for no reason. Later that evening the tragedy between the Garland and the Golden Dawn occurred in which more than 20 people lost their lives.

Of course, Moses Harvey, strolling the beach that morning in 1874, smelling the giant squid—the sweet, throat-inflaming mustard of it—would have discarded such notions as soft science. He wiped the rain from his lashes with his longest fingers. Up the beach, he saw a team of fishermen struggling with their accidental catch; their 75-foot long, two-ton catch with eyes larger than the faces of grandfather clocks—the largest eyes of any creature in the animal kingdom. The bitter metal of adrenaline rushed to Harvey's tongue. Presumably, he quickened his pace toward the yellow-jacketed fishermen, the rain in his eyes, the chill in his coat, the sand, the sea, the weather, the nets, the dead fish at his feet and the living fish in the water beyond him and, though Harvey, given the hour and temperature, did not think of ice cream at that moment, the ocean itself rolled toward him, all of its inhabitants elephantine and microscopic suspended within, like a great elemental scoop of.

ග

, DEATH BY CHOCOLATE

As Harvey stepped closer to the scene, he saw now that the fishermen's raincoats were uniformly orange—and not yellow–and, as they surrounded the fallen beast like so many scattered searchlights, the smell of it, this close, shifted to something so deeply marine it smelled *dark*–mineshaft-dark; the rotting corpses of countless failed canaries, the ones who got lost in the pitch; and something of burning tires. In this, Harvey surely began to feel faint, the cool of the rain trickling to the inside of his coat, the drops running along the lines of his body, into his armpits, over his ribcage, commingling with the anxious sweat there. He exhaled and, given the temperature, saw his breath escape him, tumble into the air toward the giant squid, graying massive on dry land, and disappear. He began to have trouble determining exactly what he was seeing–what was, and what wasn't.

The giant squid

is an umbrella classification that may encompass up to eight species.

has ten arms.

is prey to sperm whales, who house in their heads both spermaceti (a white waxy substance of uncertain biological function that humans have extracted and used in making candles, ointments, and cosmetics) and the biggest brain of any animal.

is the semimissing link between vertebrates and invertebrates as, according to Harvey, "the glassy internal pen . . . and the calcareous internal 'bone' . . . are held to foreshadow the spinal column of the higher animals."

's tentacles are adorned with subspherical suction cups, each of which can be five centimeters in diameter, possess a sharp serrated lining, and are responsible for the ring-shaped scars that are commonly found on the heads of sperm whales.

's tentacles are grouped around the beast's "beak," which resembles that of a parrot, but is way, way bigger.

's suckers are typically described as "campanulate," meaning *of a flower,* meaning *bell-shaped,* meaning *like a campanula*, the bloom which lent its name to Rapunzel, the bloom from which white latex is extracted to make the gloves worn by scientists when they dissect things like the giant squid.

's blood loses its ability to carry oxygen in warmer waters, resulting in suffocation.

is fast. Harvey tells us that the shooting of its tentacles toward its prey "is the perfection of animal mechanism . . . the most rapid motion known in the whole animal kingdom–not excepting even that of the tongue of the toad and the lizard."

has the world's largest nerve axon, or nerve fiber, or cellular jump-rope, the plaything of the dendritic schoolchildren who snort nodes of ranvier between recess and electricity class.

’s gotta lotta nerve, but is unresponsive to bad jokes.

’s eyes can be 46 centimeters in diameter, the same as that of

a beach ball

a basketball hoop

an extralarge (or “family size”) pizza

a birdbath that can hold forty adult robins

the cylinders within T. W. Worsdell’s 52-ton train engine which regularly carried twenty carriages over the steep gradients and sharp curves of the Great Eastern Railway,

the 1,900-pound balance wheel of a nineteenth-century gold-mining engine.

’s binomial nomenclature is *Architeuthis harveyi*, after, of course, the Reverend Moses.

’s pharynx is the size of an infant’s head: we see our children in it.

moves by propelling seawater through its torso (or mantle) in a rhythm that mimics human heartbeat.

’s own heart is often described as “lozenge-shaped,” something we can suck on to alleviate our sore throats.

lays her eggs—sometimes up to 50,000 at a time!—in a string that resembles a pearl necklace, torn, bouncing along the seafloor on her legs until she finds an object that she deems suitable on which to pile the mass of embryos, a process which often results in thousands of acres of seafloor to be covered with the sheen of her jellied eggs, until such an object, like a big pink shell, is found.

is carnivorous.

is the kraken's backstory.

is the largest animal without a backbone.

has been fed to dogs.

was sighted by two lighthouse keepers attacking a baby whale off the coast of Danger Point, South Africa, my wife's home country, in October 1966. With the whale's mother watching, the squid clung to the

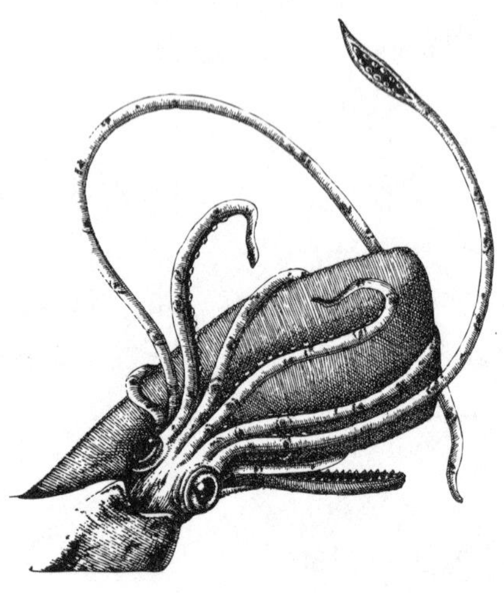

drowning calf for nearly two hours and, according to one of the lighthouse keepers, "the little whale could stay down for ten to twelve minutes, then come up. It would just have enough time to spout—only two or three seconds—and then down again."

can fuck up a sperm whale beyond sucker scars. In 1965, a Soviet whaler witnessed a battle between the two beasts. The resulting report read something like this, "задушил кита, плавающего в море с щупальца кальмара обернутые вокруг горла кита. Отрубленная голова кальмара был найден в желудке кита," which loosely translates as "the strangled whale was found floating in the sea with the squid's tentacles wrapped around the whale's throat. The squid's severed head was found in the whale's stomach." As cool as that sounds, it sounds better in Russian.

doesn't make for easy prey in any language.

three times attacked the *Brunswick*, the Royal Norwegian Navy's 15,000-ton auxiliary tanker, in the 1930s. Each time, the great beast was killed by the ship's propellers, which themselves died prematurely as a result.

three times mistook the *Brunswick* for a sperm whale, meaning that the great beast would often, as my father encouraged me to do, as I was a small and sometimes bullied child, "fight back first."

can best be captured "with all its faculties intact," via a theoretical jig that would stand over 6 feet tall, would be studded with hooks large and small, would be akin to "a man-sized cigar with a fringe of tentacles at the front end," would be fatter than most human beings, and would be baited with cut-up fish whose blood and scent would leach into the water through small perforations. Once hooked on this fat man jig, the boat's winch would "play" the beast in the way that a "killer boat" plays a whale. The squid would then be drawn alongside the boat, bathed in searchlight, and shot in the head with "a heavy rifle." This capture would be, according to the *Atlantic Advocate*'s Bruce S. Wright, "The greatest fishing thrill left on earth."

while real, can best be captured in theory.

is, in Newfoundland, nicknamed "sea arrow" by the same fishermen who use it for bait.

is, in its larval state, weak and slitlike.

appears, underwater, to be translucent.

fresh out of the water is a dusky red. After a while, it will turn pure white.

's eating habits were, until very recently, a complete

mystery, as all specimens were found, strangely, with empty stomachs.

is big and hungry and can ingest fish even larger than itself, stalking its prey with its arms curved over its head, hiding the length of the tentacles, until proximity dictates the springing forward, the exploding arms, some thick as a mizzenmast, the lashing prey, the smothering, the engulfing, the suckers, as Harvey himself says, "perhaps twelve-hundred at once, sinking into the flesh . . . some the size of pot-lids . . . feeling like so many mouths devouring him at the same time . . . seeming to drink the very blood," as the squid slowly drags the meal into its beak, its huge stomach turning bright red with the blood of the fish.

have been described as "using light patterns, colors, and postures as a means of communication. They didn't just turn red or pink or yellow; ripples of color would wash across their bodies. And they would contort their arms into elaborate arrangements—sometimes balling them together, or holding them above their heads like flamenco dancers."

inspires scientists to go to extreme measures to capture it on film, such as the time Smithsonian Institution zoologist and Transylvania University graduate (and Captain Ahab-bearded) Clyde Roper and his crew attached a camera to the back of a whale (which can't be easy), and retrieved some killer whale footage, but nothing of the giant squid.

allows so many pet owners to name their cats Architeuthis.

was the basis, in nineteenth-century Japan, for a "squid show," which, according to Harvey, "consists of a series of figures carved in wood, the size of life, and cleverly coloured ... [In one] was a group of women bathing in the sea; one of them had been caught in the folds of a giant cuttle-fish; the others, in alarm, were escaping, leaving their companion to her fate. The cuttle-fish was represented on a large scale—its eyes, eyelids, and mouth being made to move simultaneously by a man inside the head."

was spotted one night by A. G. Starkey, a World War II British Admiralty trawler, who reported "as I gazed, fascinated, a circle of green light glowed in my area of illumination. This green unwinking orb I suddenly realized was an eye. The surface of the water undulated with some strange disturbance. Gradually I realized that I was gazing at almost point-blank range at a huge squid," whereupon he strolled the 175-foot-long deck, bow to stern, and saw the tail breach the former, and the tentacles the latter.

is distinguished from other known cephalopods by "the most remarkable anatomical character observed": the form and arrangement, as if symphonic, of the teeth on its "lingual ribbon."

has paired organs of equilibrium and detection called statocysts. These detect both linear and angular acceleration. These organs have a greater likelihood of fossilization than other structures and are used to both identify fossil species and to age the giant squid.

has no idea that the prefix *stato-* means *remaining.*

may be the evolutionary stepping-stone from the mollusks to the fishes.

even at 1,000 pounds, is known to jump 10 feet out of the water, earning it, in northern Newfoundland, the local moniker "jumper."

when swimming with others of their kind, have been described by fishermen as "looking like a shower of meteors against the blue depths; turning upward in graceful lines, their white sides glisten like a nebula of silvery stars and as quickly disappear."

is a Web design company based in St. Paul, Minnesota, with this motto: "Your goals could be giant squids—things that you thought were imaginary, but are in fact quite real."

is a self-proclaimed metal-progressive rock band based in San Francisco, California whose song titles include "Neonate," "Ampullae of Lorenzini," "Monster in the Creek," and "Octopus" (a Syd Barrett cover).

is an audio lab specializing in "miniature stereo and mono, cardioid, and omnidirectional microphones." They also specialize in their "own make of small, durable . . . microphones that can be [creepily and] discretely mounted."

is, according to squidsquid.com, easily insulted. According to the same source, effective insults range from "Your mama is so fat, your daddy thought he was attacking a submarine" (offensive), to "Your prehensile spermatophore-depositing tube looks short" (abusive).

has three hearts.

if male, has a penis that, when erect, can be as long as the mantle (torso), head, and arms combined. As such, according to A. I. Arkhipkin's and V. V. Laptikhovsky's article "Observation of Penis Elongation in *Onykia ingens*: Implications for Spermatophore Transfer in Deep-Water Squid," published in the June 30, 2010, issue of *Journal of Molluscan Studies*, our beast possesses the "greatest known penis length relative to body size of all mobile animals, second in the entire animal kingdom only to certain sessile barnacles" whose dicks, obviously, are way smaller.

is a letterpress in Astoria, Queens, New York City, specializing in custom business cards, posters, wedding invitations, and stationery, bearing an evilly smiling androgynous jack-o'-lantern atop a female torso readying to flash her gourdy boobs à la Mardi Gras.

in Greece is garnished with parsley.
in Mexico with habañero peppers.
in Portugal with bell pepper.
in Sardinia with garlic and olive oil.
in Albania with squash.
in Turkey with tomato.
in Malta with capers.
in Spain with mayonnaise.
in Korea with mustard and pillard leaves.
in Slovenia with cheese and Swiss chard.
in China with rice.
in Russia with onion.
in India with tamarind.
in Japan with its fermented innards.
in the Philippines with its own fat.
in the Mediterranean with its own ink.

is served grilled or baked (diner's choice) in a ginger-infused soy sauce at Santa Clara, California's Hatcho Restaurant.

is for sale, in all of its burgundy-colored plush 12"l. x 4"w. x 4"h. x 4"dia. glory in the gift shop of the National Museum of Natural History for $25.00 to nonmembers, and $22.50 to members. The stuffed animal has garnered only one online review, which lists nothing under CONS, and under PROS lists these four "adjectives": cute, long-lasting, realistic (!), squidtastic.

is for sale, under the ad titled "lots of Artificial Squid for Sale," on the Sword Fishing Central Forum, by a guy whose username is RUSTBUCKET LINES-IN, whose sales pitch involves "I have a whole box load," and "make your own teasers and such," and "here are the squid and colors I have," and "dirt cheap," and "very durable."

is a cake, according to the blog Cloth and Fodder, which insists that the dessert need be white-chocolate-based and include in its list of ingredients a "toy boat" as a "reference point."

is, in a frightening coincidence, featured in cartoon form on the front of a Real M.O.B. Apparel Squid Comic T-shirt holding an ice-cream cone (the shirt's descriptive ad caption reads: *A sweet little cephalopod enjoying his ice cream*).

is a character in Team Club Penguin Cheats, some sort of game-playing group whose mission, with every sentence in it self-referential and rife with jargon only members can comprehend, eludes me.

is, according to David Klinghoffer's article on recovering the wisdom of the Hebrew Bible, "If the Children of Israel Were Giant Squid," a perfect analogous tool for understanding the "subtext" of Psalm 137.

is, according to a 2004 Reuters report, a perfect, if unwitting, drug mule. In Lima, "Peruvian police say they have seized nearly 1,540 pounds (700 kilograms) of cocaine hidden in frozen giant squid bound for Mexico and the United States."

is, according to Harvey, the same thing as the mythical Sea Serpent. "A double-headed, double-spined serpent seventy tons in weight, with something like the mane of a horse washing about the neck, is too much for this sceptical generation . . . and should this theory be sustained, it would follow that I have been successful in unmasking both, and I should have done greater things than I knew . . . and if I am in error, I am astray in good company."

is the basis for one of my favorite boyhood articles printed in the May 1983 issue of my second favorite boyhood magazine (after *Zoobooks*), *Boys' Life*, which includes what was my single favorite sentence for the remainder of 1983, a sentence that revealed, in its simple concision, a world far larger than the one I inhabited, a sentence that evoked something beyond me—a future perhaps, some gargantuan adulthood that hung just out of reach, a sentence that I repeated to Poppa Dave when Poppa Dave still had three years to live, lying on his hairy chest and Jewish mafia bling *chai* necklace on his and Grandma Ruth's screened-in porch of their Palm Springs Phase II Margate, Florida, retirement condo, the interior of which was all peach and coral and the kind of silver that reflected your face back to you in that distorted, funhouse sort of way that made your eyes look bigger than they really were: "There are some who are convinced that species of giant squid exist that are still unknown to scientists," after which Poppa Dave exhaled a mouthful of postdinner cigar smoke, and, lifting the lip of his white wife-beater undershirt, asked me, seven-years-old, "Did I ever tell you how I got this scar?"

is right in front of Moses Harvey in 1874, the beast dead, but still somehow heaving, a trick of sunlight, the sun itself fat over the ocean, breaking through the sky's film as if from some Great Beyond, like Poppa Dave's enlarged heart, which the Long Island coroner who pronounced him dead in 1986 called *giant,* the result perhaps of too many cigars, too many inflated tales told to his grandson, too many diner scoops of his rich and ever-favorite flavor, promising, right there in its title, our demise.

ᔓ

, TURTLE TRACKS

"I haven't ever seen an account of the transportation of the squid or the logistics of his draping it in the bathtub," says Joan Ritcey, the head of the Centre for Newfoundland Studies at the Memorial University Libraries (a university whose motto is *Provehito in altum* or "Launch forth into the depths"), a dark-haired, middle-aged woman who favors white embroidered blouses that seem souvenirs from vacations to locales that demand the adjective *indigenous*, "but you might find something on these matters if you read everything that Harvey published on the topic."

"Everything?" I ask.

Ritcey says nothing.

"You mean everything about Harvey obtaining the squid in question, or everything about Harvey and his obsession with marine biology?" I ask.

"Everything," Ritcey says.

Her elbows are pressed into her torso as if sewn there. They never leave her body, never flap out into the air. I wonder if she's kidding.

The incomplete bibliography, imposingly titled in brick-red Times New Roman, "Works of the Rev. Dr. Moses Harvey," compiled by Ritcey's own Memorial University Libraries, the ambitious, perhaps delusional mandate of which, Ritcey is compelled to tell me, "is to collect all materials relating to Newfoundland and Labrador," numbers 449 pages, and includes (as it's a bibliography) no actual text, merely article names, dates and places of publication. If each page lists on average six or seven entries, and if each entry encompasses on average 4 or 5 pages, and if each special collections article would cost, to a "non-affiliated person" like me, anywhere from (after doing the currency conversion) US$5.00 to US$41.64 depending on article length, rarity, and availability, then in order to "read everything that Harvey published," I would potentially have to hew through 3,143 articles and lecture transcripts, numbering 15,715 pages, costing me, a nonaffiliated person, approximately (factoring the mean per article price of US$23.32) US$73,294.76.

I am daunted by this. Regardless, Ms. Ritcey seems very nice and tells me that should I require permissions to publish any images (like the one of the squid draped over the tub), to just let her know.

To gel with the "one step at a time" mentality that my psychologist friend informs me that I am in dire need of gelling with, I decide to check out the titles of Harvey's articles published in 1873 and 1874, in the days leading up to his obtaining of the squid, and the days thereafter. Here are some of the seafaring ones (selected list):

Another Fishery Dispute: Aug. 5, 1873, Royal Gazette

Arctic adventures, the story of the Polaris, a voyage of two-thousand miles on an ice-floe, a thrilling narrative of the wonderful escape: May 21, 1873, Evening Post

Beaver in Newfoundland: Aug. 9, 1873, Cdn. Ill. News

Cable monopoly–Newfoundland coming to the front–The fisheries–Freaks of the lightning–False alarm–The weather: August 9, 1873, Citizen

Confederation adjourned sine die–Telegraph Company, important clause in their charter–Seal fishery–Death of Inspector Foley: May 6, 1873, Citizen

Devil Fish: December 6, 1873, Morning Chronicle

Devil-fish caught–Extraordinary capture by Logie Bay fishermen–The head of the monster struck off and the whole now in pickle in St. John's–Interest of scientific men in these gigantic cuttles: Dec. 23, 1873, World (N.Y.)

Devil-fish in Conception Bay: Nov. 21, 1873, Morning Chronicle

Devil-fish–Size of the gigantic cuttle-fish–Agassiz on the subject–The political outlook–Wreck of the S.S. Robert Lowe–Another hoax

Devils of the sea–Capture in Newfoundland of monster octopus–Coming to New York–Victor Hugo's marvellous fictions verified by fact–Cephalopods of the Atlantic–"Blue Nose" fishermen in deadly conflict with a massive squid

And so on, and so on, until I feel like I've tumbled down the rabbit hole, but am too slow for the task, the next insufficient turtle in line, mismatched with the speed required to accomplish, following the cold well-paved pathway, littered with rank pecans, chocolate, caramel, until I get off-trail and can't find my way back to the comfort of the.

~

SO WHY THE GIANT SQUID, AFTER ALL? HOW DID this particular beast become the basis for our kraken? Why is it that when we think of the proverbial sea monster, the image most of us generate is one that most closely resembles the giant squid? Why is this animal the recipient of our need to mythologize? The giant squid is real, yet somehow remains, simultaneously, in the realm of myth. What combinatory cocktail does the giant squid embody that allows it, to the human world, to straddle both worlds: the actual and the legendary? Maybe it's merely a fusion of its size and its rarity.

It's big, of course, but studies show that the giant squid population is fairly widespread, and they have been sighted in all of our oceans. They are rare only in polar and tropical latitudes.

The Knysna African elephant, by comparison, is both much bigger and much more rare. It weighs nearly twenty-two times more than the giant squid, and according to studies conducted by a collection of wildlife scientists working for South Africa National Parks, there is no evidence that more than one—*one*—Knysna elephant still exists today. (In 1874, the year Moses Harvey found and photographed his giant squid, there were about 500

Knysna elephants in existence; by 1901, the year Moses Harvey died, the Knysna elephant population had already dwindled to about 30, due to decimation by woodcutters and hunters; their numbers dwindled to 9 by 1976, the year I was born, and to 3 by 1986, the year Poppa Dave died.)

Still, the Knysna elephant does not serve as the blueprint for any of our mythological creatures. There must be another factor besides size and rarity. Perhaps the ocean has something to do with it: size, rarity, ocean. Is that the cocktail? Do we have to incorporate the element of the sea, the bulk of the Earth of which we're not a part?

But still: in our oceans, there are creatures bigger and rarer. The ocean sunfish, or mola mola (Latin for *millstone millstone*—so named for its grayish stony flesh, repeated perhaps due to its surprising size), can weigh up to six times as much as a fully-grown giant squid, and is less widespread.

Blue whales are far more endangered (Dr. Jay Barlow of the National Oceanic and Atmospheric Administration, the swaggering mission statement of which claims, "Our reach goes from the surface of the sun to the depths of the ocean floor," estimates that there are few more than 10,000 blue whales left, worldwide), and are approximately 2.5 times longer than the giant squid and 656 times heavier.

Even the oarfish is longer than the giant squid by about 13 feet, and human sightings of this live fish are so few that our knowledge of their distribution depends on records of those washed ashore, dead. In fact, the first confirmed sighting of the oarfish alive and swimming at depth occurred as recently as July 2008. At least the Japanese mythologize the oarfish, though, believing it to be the messenger from Ryūjin's, the dragon sea god's, undersea palace of Ryūgū-jō, and the harbinger of earthquakes. It is said that one day within the palace walls is the equivalent of a human century. In Ryūgū-jō, Moses Harvey first photographed the giant squid the day before yesterday.

Oarfish, sunfish, blue whale, elephant. All of them should have the giant squid beat. Do we feel compelled to mythologize the beast for the same reasons I feel compelled to mythologize my Poppa Dave, who never should have lived beyond infancy, but grew to live through the Army and Dixieland jazz and a marriage to a woman who would later, as my grandmother, dye her hair orange, and reported affiliations with the Jewish mafia and a penchant for flamboyant clothes like pink and yellow plaid pants and red alligator shoes and white fedoras with brown feathers coming out of them and flamboyant cars like his infamous Gucci Cadillac–painted white with gold-plated hubcaps and plush Gucci upholstery papering the outer roof and inner seats—which allowed him, he always bragged, the A-OK hand-sign from a cadre of New York City pimps whenever he and Grandma Ruth stopped at a traffic light and which, after Poppa Dave died in 1986, my dad sold to a Long Island dentist for $200?

In 1916, the year Poppa Dave was born, the mortality rate for all infants born prematurely was 21.2. Given that Poppa Dave was born way, way prematurely, that rate was quadrupled. Out of 100 infants born under the same circumstances that Poppa Dave was, about 85 would have died within the first few days of life outside the womb. In 1916, there were approximately 438,000 premature births reported in the U.S. If all of them matched Poppa Dave's eagerness and earlyhood, that means 372,300 dead babies. If all of these babies were, as Poppa Dave was, diagnosed with Extremely Low Birth Weight (ELBW), which means less than 2 pounds, 3 ounces, then the weight of all of those 372,300 ELBW babies who didn't make it would equal that of 1,220 giant squid, 203 sunfish, 55 Knysna elephants, or 1.86 blue whales. All of those human deaths. One complete blue whale.

Mythology as cloak, and winter jacket, as blanket, as salve, as handkerchief at Poppa Dave's funeral where I, ten years old, threw a single and ceremonial shovelful of earth into his open grave, where it thudded and echoed on the surface of his coffin, scattered into such small sand over its sides. My cousins followed suit. Then my uncle. Then my dad. I remember no flies. Afterward, in the funeral home, smoked salmon and small Jewish sweets; I watched out the window as a bulldozer, driven by a man in a sleeveless shirt, finished the job in under a second. One human shovelful of dirt into a grandfather's grave is to the weight of a 1916 ELBW baby, as the bulldozer's capacity is to the weight of the giant squid.

Until '86, though, prematurely born Poppa Dave beat the evolutionary odds and natural selection process to produce my dad, who also should never have been born, who grew to produce me, who also should never have... and who grew to boyhood to sit on his Poppa's lap and lay on his Poppa's chest on that screened-in porch of the Palm Springs Phase II Margate, Florida, retirement condo, as Poppa Dave peeled off his undershirt, shook the boy off, turned his back and asked the rapt seven-year-old, "Did I ever tell you how I got this scar?"

I remember examining the puffed circle of pinkish-brown on Poppa Dave's lower back, just to the left of his spine. It hung there the size of a nickel.

"You can touch it," he said, and I was relieved. He knew me. He knew I wanted to touch it. It was warm and smooth and smelled of cigar tobacco and musk aftershave. Or maybe that was his breath, his neck, his triple-chin rough with stubble.

While it was still under my finger, he said, "I was swimming in the Pacific Ocean off the coast of Japan, and one of those big squids got me. Wrapped its tentacles right around me. But you know how I can float [and I did: backfloating and reading, backfloating and reading in so many public pools]. So it only got one sucker on me, right there," he said, putting his hand over mine, which was over his scar, "before I floated away . . . Ask your grandma. She was there too."

And my grandma rolled her eyes and said something about his smoking too many cigars.

And my little sister told me that Poppa Dave told her that the scar was a result of a rhinoceros attack in Africa.

And Poppa Dave told me stories of huge octopi that would suck sailors into their mouths where they would live like marbles on octopus tonsils for the rest of their days, forming culture and colony inside the great beast.

"They built bakeries in there," he would say, "and roads."

I would have delicious nightmares and, the next night, ask for more. And the next night, he might tell me that he got the scar while escaping from such a monster, that its suction cup sucked out a bit of his marrow, and even a knuckle of bone from his spine. And he would tell me that I inherited my own bad back, my own malformed spine, my own spina bifida occulta from him; that this affliction stemmed not from the drugs my father abused while conceiving me, but from some microscopic amniotic version of a giant squid that grew inside of him after the attack, replacing the excised marrow, which he then passed on to my father, which was then passed on to me, and which I will, he stressed with dejected eyes, pass on to my own male children. As a child, I imagined such a thing swimming with my fetal self inside my mother's womb, telling me secrets, acting the bad influence.

And I wish, in the days leading to his death, I reminded him of this story, but I just closed myself off in my bedroom, a collection of states away, and read and reread *The Amazing Spider-Man* #129: the first appearance of the Punisher, one of my all-time faves.

Grandma Ruth, then pre-Alzheimer's, told me that Poppa Dave received the scar after being shot in the back by German soldiers during the Battle of the Bulge in World War II.

And I wonder if, when facedown in the forests of the Ardennes Mountains, he confused the soil there with the floor of the Brooklyn tenement of his childhood, if he expected Dorothy, his mother, to approach fat-armed and force-feed him.

He was counted among the 88,000 U.S. casualties during that battle and was unable to walk for months afterward, was told by Army doctors that he'd never walk again, but he did that too, beat the odds, became strong enough to break the ribs of my grandma while hugging her after returning home from the war, and strong enough to hold a saxophone again, the same one he played when he wrote a song about a squid and wooed the girl who was to become my grandmother, who was to become the one to tell me the truth behind the myth, just before losing herself to the ocean of a deteriorating brain.

~

OF COURSE, THERE'S THE COMMON STORY OF the so many questions I never got to ask my grandparents before they died. I remember, soon after securing my driver's license, after dropping my friends off, I would speed along the suburban Chicago streets in my mom's 1986 Plymouth Voyager minivan—maroon with faux wood trim—and pop in the "Living Years" cassette single by Mike and the Mechanics, that shamelessly saccharine song about a dying father and rebirth and yadda yadda, and I would cry and wonder about the meaning of it all as best a sixteen-year-old can, before returning to my bedroom and the comfort of ogling the Alyssa Milano-in-a-semi-buttoned-cardigan pinup on the wall.

~

PREPARING THE GHOST

The backward motion is that which is most graceful and natural in the squid.

—Moses Harvey,
The Devilfish in Newfoundland Waters (1874)

ᘓ

IT'S ONLY NATURAL THAT I REMEMBER POPPA Dave, teaching me piano as a child. The white piano on Ruthie's bloody red carpet, and Poppa Dave teaching me with his fat musician's fingers, the Yiddish song "Sha, Sha der Rebe Geyt," and I would sing with him, not realizing I was saying, loudly, *Shh, shh, the rabbi is about to dance again . . .*

And the way he would ritualistically eat four Carvel Brown Bonnet ice-cream cones from the freezer always on the first nights of my family visits to New York, and how Ruthie would yell at him because of *all the sugar, Dave, the sugar!* and how *you're killing yourself!* and how *you're gonna make a mess on the carpet!* and how he never made a mess, and his saxophones collecting dust in my parents' storage closet, his diabetes and insulin injections, which he kept, when visiting my family in Chicago, in the same cabinet as the dog food, and how he struggled to walk uphill in amusement parks, and that dirt I threw into his grave, and the thud it made on the coffin lid, and how I remember no flies at his funeral, and how if there are no flies, something's not dead.

&

Myth as a bird in a backyard.
Myth as our bodies.
Myth as the body.
Myth as a ghost in a jacket.
Myth as the farmer and the windmill.
Myth as the niece who feels kinship with the lizard.

&

THE RED BRICK ROWHOUSES OF DEVON ROW ARE now painted this soft, awful doctor's-office waiting-room purple. The kind of color meant to soothe before something painful comes–the drawing of bags of blood. The paint is peeling and I look left and I look right, and something–not a heart–beating inside me says "You're clear," and I yank off a piece of paint the size of my forearm, stash it in my windbreaker pocket, and see the original brick beneath, and I touch it, and it feels like the original brick beneath. Down the street, a white stretch limousine pulls into the U-shaped driveway of the Sheraton and idles. A young mother drags her daughter by the arm into LeMoine's School of Esthetics and Hair Design, the daughter clutching a foil tree-frog balloon. The balloon gets caught outside, and I can hear the girl's scream halved by the closing door as she's forced to release the ribbon. Next door to the school is the Wig Shop, the side of which has been spray-painted in black, SCHIAVO—*slave* in Italian. There's a frog in the sky.

Each of the rowhouses, except for 3 Devon Row, have been broken into a slew of apartments, the huge wooden doorways now adorned with dozens of tiny nailed-on mailboxes and a confetti of doorbells. Only Moses Harvey's old home remains an enormous single-family. I climb the three steps. I smell the door of it, the doorknob. I look for old fingerprints. I scratch at the paint. I swallow. I nod to the pedestrians passing on the sidewalk just below, carrying shopping bags, or their lovers' hands, or bottles, or nothing. I swallow harder, ring the doorbell, but I can't hear it. I wait. That thing is still beating inside me. I crouch and push open the heavy brass mail slot. Still, it remains open, pushed-in. I can't angle my fingers properly inside to get it closed again. I've given myself away. The huge half-moon window above the door rattles in its base. In the winter, this must be such a cold house. I peer through the mail slot, see only a mess of houseplants. I ring the bell again. Wait. Beat. A man behind me with paint-stained hands eating a drumstick that looks too large to be chicken. The ocean. The window. The peeling paint. I push a note with my phone number and email address and a brief abstract of my Moses Harvey mission through the slot into the tangle of leaves, imploring the owner for a walk-through. I turn, the house having left some sheen on my skin like soap scum in soft water.

Across the street, watching me, two old men in fishing jackets on orange chairs drinking from paper bags in a half-opened garage. Behind them, a refrigerator hums with the ocean. The one on the left raises his bag to me. "Ain't nobodys evers home, eh boy?" he says.

ᘓ

I WONDER IF, WHEN HE CAME UPON THAT GIANT squid that 1874 morning, Reverend Moses Harvey, as shocked as Poppa Dave postbullet, thought of what brought him here to this doorstep, if he remembered his own childhood in Armagh, Ireland, the least populated settlement to be granted the designation (by Queen Elizabeth II in 1994) of *city* in the entire country. If one grows up in a smallest city, and later becomes obsessed with an animal that has *giant* in its name, is this an understandable, even directly traceable, example of classic male overcompensation? We come from small, so we mythologize the giant? Was the giant squid Harvey's midlife crisis sports car? His affair with a twenty-two-year-old personal trainer? The third wheel in Moses and Sarah's marriage?

Were the seeds of this obsession sown somehow, in their embryonic stage, in Armagh?

Perhaps Harvey's obsession was informed by a fabulous carnival barkerism, the likes of which were rendered on many an Irish broadsheet, like this mysterious one dating from 1673:

> A Wonderful Fish or Beast that was lately killed... as it came of its own accord to Him out of the sea to the Shore, where he was alone on horseback at the Harbour's Mouth of Dingle-Icoush, which had two heads and Ten horns, and upon Eight of the said Horns about 800 Buttons or the resemblance of Little Coronets; and in each of them a set of Teeth, the said Body was bigger than a Horse and was 19 Foot Long Horns and all, the great Head thereof Carried only the said ten Horns and two very large Eyes, And the little Head thereof carried a wonderful strange mouth and two tongues in it...

Or perhaps his enthusiasm is untraceable, confusing even to him, or perhaps his enthusiasm attached itself at birth, ink seeping evilly into broadsheet...

1820: Harvey is born in March, two months after George III (yes, the crazy one, whose craziness is said to have been the result of the blood disorder porphyria, the symptoms of which include seizures, vomiting, hallucinations, paranoia, and the unfortunate intestinal volleying between constipation and diarrhea), King of the UK and Ireland, dies. In the days leading up to his death, he succumbed to total blindness, deafness, and dementia. He died at eighty-one, and reigned for fifty-nine of those years. He left behind a profound collection of scientific instruments, most of which are now housed in London's Science Museum. He was obsessed with the cosmos and feverishly funded (though his advisors advised him against it) the development of astronomer William Herschel's giant telescope—40 feet long and the biggest ever built—which was later responsible for discovering Uranus, which Herschel dubbed *Georgium Sidus*, or George's Star. He lost the support of the American Revolutionary colonists, who dubbed him, the King of Uranus, a tyrant. His legacy is one of insanity and obsession, of giant things and the planets and of naming. Under these stars came into the world Moses Harvey.

1825: Harvey, a toddler, playing outside in Armagh, about 50 miles inland from the Irish Sea, has no idea yet that, not too far away, in England, William H. James just invented the first SCUBA system, which of course had some growing pains (attached to the original apparatus were such things as insufficient air hose tether, depth restrictions, and oxygen poisoning). The young Harvey would not stay in the dark long.

1831: As Harvey turns eleven, Charles Darwin prepares to depart the coast of England via the HMS *Beagle* in search of unique species in places such as Tierra del Fuego and the Galápagos Islands. Years later, Harvey would eulogize Darwin in the April 27, 1882, issue of Dublin's *Evening Herald.*

Did Harvey know that, just a few weeks before his birth, Russian explorers Fabian Gottlieb von Bellingshausen and Mikhail Petrovich Lazarev became the first human beings to lay eyes on Antarctica, and that, years later, during Harvey's own lifetime, the most giant of the giant squids was nicknamed the Antarctic squid?

That, nineteen days after his birth, the HMS *Beagle*, which will eleven years later carry Darwin to history, is launched?

That, eight months after Harvey's birth, a whale sinks the ship *Essex* of Nantucket, and the survivors resorted to cannibalism?

That, one month after Harvey's birth, John Keats published "Ode on Melancholy," which includes the lines, "Then glut thy sorrow on a morning rose. / Or on the rainbow of the salt sand-wave" and in which Keats begs his reader not to "... twist / Wolf's-bane, tight-rooted, for its poisonous wine"?

And that wolf's-bane is a plant and that "poisonous wine" has been interpreted as the ocean, and that Keats may have been telling Harvey not to squeeze the ocean from the earth, that the ocean will kill you?

That Joseph Banks, British naturalist, botanist, and inspiration to both Harvey and Darwin, died less than three months after Harvey's birth?

That, in 1899, less than two years before Harvey's death, a German teuthologist (a cephalopod expert or squid enthusiast) on his Valdivia expedition, spotted some unusual squid in the water, about which he said:

> Among the marvels of coloration which the animals of the deep sea exhibited to us nothing can be even distantly compared with the hues of these organs. One would think that the body was adorned with a diadem of brilliant gems. The middle organs of the eyes shone with ultramarine blue, the lateral ones with a pearly sheen. Those towards the front of the lower surface of the body gave off a ruby-red light, while those behind were snow-white or pearly, except the median one, which was sky-blue. It was indeed a glorious spectacle.

That Sir Thomas Cochrane, a Navy man, became, when Moses Harvey turned five, the governor of Newfoundland, and stationed troops in St. John's, a stone's throw from the house that Moses and Sarah would later occupy?

What we do know is that Harvey knew that Sir Thomas Cochrane, according to the 1883 book *Newfoundland, the Oldest British Colony: Its History, Its Present Condition, and Its Prospects in the Future*, co-written by Joseph Hatton (a journalist for the UK's *Sunday Times*) and Reverend Moses Harvey (!),

> saw the necessity of roads ... and his Government was rendered forever memorable by the construction of the first roads ever made in the island. One of these extended to Portugal Cove.... Along these highways settlements and cultivation crept steadily, and neat farm-houses were erected.... Up to this date, though the country had been inhabited for centuries, the construction of roads had never been attempted, as it was considered that for fishing-stations the sea furnished sufficient means of inter-communication, and the settlement of the country was not contemplated.

Newfoundland saw its first road only in 1825, and the period fisherfolk were outraged at the appearance of said road, bellowing, among other rants, "They are making *roads* in Newfoundland! Next thing, they'll be having carriages and driving about!"

As a result of these roads and driving-about carriages, trade flourished in the region. The seal-fishing industry in St. John's increased their employment to 3,000 men, and their fleet to 125 ships. Conception Bay, made famous in Harvey's article "Devil-fish in Conception Bay," written ten years earlier for the *Morning Chronicle*, which detailed his sighting of a giant squid there, contributed 218 ships and nearly 5,000 men to the now-booming seal-fishing trade. With the money, Conception Bay sprouted factories: chocolate ones and antelope glove ones, ones for leaky rubber boots and hockey sticks and glass eyes.

We can infer that these roads were made of dirt and stone, and that humans traveled them on foot, and that humans traveled them on horseback, and that humans traveled them via stagecoach, and that Cochrane's road from St. John's to Portugal Cove, the road that Moses Harvey felt he must highlight in his book about Newfoundland, is the same road that allowed the three fishermen, Little Tommy Picco, Theophilus Picco, and Daniel Squires, to bring the 19-foot tentacle of the giant squid to Moses Harvey's house that October 26, 1873, a Sunday, as Moses and Sarah were just sitting down to their boiled potatoes.

He had just that morning delivered a sermon, which

maybe referenced the Devil-fish; a sermon which was, as usual, "marked by perspicacity, force and metaphysical reasoning, the wonderful powers of illustration and simile." The giant squid was like the devil. He had not yet considered that soon, in less than five years, he would have to step down from the church, as first his hearing, and then his voice would abandon him. His sermons were numbered. His similes finite. He thought of his past sermons, their themes–"The Harmony of Science and Religion"; "Egypt and Its Monuments"; "The Poetry of the Bible"–and tried to make them cohere into a mass that could make sense of his life, the things he'd endured. Possibly, he was staring at that road, the road that would allow him to transport giant squid from the sea to his bathroom. And the road and the road. The road as throat, and the road as thin remedy to a forthcoming voicelessness.

Part Two

THE MERE FABRICATIONS OF A DISTORTED MIND

CALAMARI, THE ITALIAN WORD FOR *SQUIDS*, HAS long been a staple food source in the Mediterranean, but took a bit longer to catch on in North America where now, along with the buffalo wing, the potato skin, the jalapeño popper, and the mozzarella stick, it dominates the appetizer sections of menus at establishments both gourmet and shitty, served alongside dipping sauces that range from lavender aioli to balsamic vinaigrette to tartar to marinara sauce.

Until somewhat recently, fishermen along North America's eastern seaboard used the calamari they caught as bait. If they had enough bait, they would discard the squids back into the sea. According to the *New York Times*, "Even up to [1981], squid fetched fishermen barely 10 cents a pound. Today the price is more than [$2] a pound and squid, or calamari, as it is increasingly being called, has become fancy fare..."

The popularity of squid on North American menus is said to have begun as a trial-and-error experiment by the Cornell Cooperative Extension, whose mission is, among other things, "to improve New York State communities through partnerships... in the areas of agriculture and food systems..." Long Island fishermen in the 1970s and '80s had "taken a hard hit... as the marine stocks traditionally depended on flounder and cod... but these are greatly reduced in numbers. So there has been much legislation to prohibit their over harvesting," the CCE encouraged "fishermen to remain in business by going after underexploited and underfished species... to literally stay afloat."

The Long Island Fisheries Assistance Program got on board with the CCE, and soon afterward, so did the Empire State Development program, and soon after that, so did the Economic Development Administration of the federal Commerce Department. And since the movement went federal, the movement went national. Restaurants who couldn't buy as much haddock and cod and flounder and other overfished species as they were used to were encouraged by local distributors and the feds alike to replace such items with squid. Chefs were encouraged to treat the squid as they would any other fish in order to foster any kind of familiarity with the customers, who, widely in North America, at least, prefer to take their fish encased in breading and deep-fried with a dipping sauce.

Squeamish and skeptical restaurant owners believed such a large meal-sized portion of a heretofore uncommon and forbidding ingredient might scare away customers, so they began, as a trial-run, offering it in smaller portions as an appetizer. The CCE, along with the other state and federal programs involved, encouraged both fishermen and restaurants to call the ingredient (for human consumption) by its Italian name, as it's known along large sections of the Mediterranean, correctly believing that the word evokes a sense of European exoticism that the word *squid* decidedly does not. The CCE knew that what we name something determines whether or not we will eat it. They set out to actively "tap into" and change "consumers' tastes," and they pulled it off.

Richard Lofstadt, president of Long Island Seafood Export Inc. declares, "We realized that in order to make money we had to move into exporting what was available and at the same time in demand. Squid turned out to be the most plentiful. Through the assistance program we got money to buy a state-of-the-art squid-skinning machine. We used to be able to skin about 300 pounds a day by hand. That was with 10 to 15 people working.

With the machine we skin about 3,000 pounds of squid for daily packaging."

"Changing ethnicity . . . may be a factor for the increase . . . in popularity. Asian immigrants, one of the fastest growing groups of newcomers [to North America], use squid widely," the *New York Times* reports.

"In 1989, the total [sales of squid nationwide] was 127 million [pounds]. In 1994, sales . . . totaled 215 million pounds . . ." While, nationally speaking, this seemed like a whole bunch, Japan, as far back as 1980, was harvesting over 600 million *tons* (or 1,200,000,000,000 pounds) of squid each year. If a typical calamari appetizer includes a quarter-pound of squid (not including the weight of breading, and accoutrements), then Japan alone, way back in 1980, was pulling enough squid to make 4,800,000,000,000 plates of the stuff for T.G.I. Friday's. That's four trillion eight hundred billion calamari appetizers. In Japan alone. Every year. If, once cleaned and cut and portioned and breaded, and once all lemon wedges were sliced, and all accompanying sauces prepared and spooned into ramekins, and all green-leaf lettuce garnishes washed and plated, it would still take the equivalent of 63,400,000 years to deep-fry that much calamari to the desired golden brown. Sixty-three million four hundred thousand years ago, during the Cretaceous-Tertiary period of geologic time, it is presumed that the asteroid that ignited the extinction of the dinosaurs struck the earth. The carbon in the earth's crust liquefied. Sunlight was obliterated. Photosynthesis ceased. Mosasaurs died, and plesiosaurs died, and pterosaurs died, and invertebrates died, and plants died, and insects died. Marsupials disappeared from North America. Save for nautiloids and coleoids–octopods, cuttlefish, and squids–all species of the Cephalopoda class went extinct. It would be approximately another 63,200,000 years until humans walked the earth, and another 199,950 years after that until the modern deep-fryer was invented.

Every year.

᪥

EMPEROR DOMETIAN OF ROME SENTENCED ST. John the Apostle to death by oil. He was plunged into a cauldron of boiling fat and, as the myth tells it, emerged unhurt. The same cannot be said for the squid.

᪥

DR. CLYDE ROPER (SMITHSONIAN INSTITUTION zoologist, Transylvania University graduate, and that guy who attached the camera to the back of the whale in a failed but awesome attempt to capture some giant-squid footage) claims that he "can cook calamari more ways than you'd care to hear."

~

SQUID CORPSES, EVEN WHEN COOKED, RETAIN their sexual reflexes and have been known to inseminate our mouths. After eating calamari (in a preparation in which Roper is likely proficient), a South Korean woman reported experiencing "severe pain" and a "pricking foreign-body sensation" in her mouth. From her tongue, inner cheeks, gums, throat, her doctor excised "twelve small, white, spindle-shaped, bug-like organisms." These were spermatophores, which possess seriously tenacious ejaculatory apparati, and a cementlike body, which allows for their attachment to materials like the tongue, inner cheeks, gums . . .

This occurrence is inspiring some scientists to ask, "Does the pain that occurs when spermatophores inject themselves into human mucosa mean that insemination is painful for female squid? It's quite possible."

~

Myth as quite possible.

Myth as commodity, as bought and sold, as served with a side of potato salad.

Myth, in Portugal, encourages the mosquito to eat leather and turn into a flesh-eating cow.

Myth, in India, inspires the tribe to receive all nec-

> essary sustenance from the smells of food, particularly the apple, and, when traveling, to carry the apple with them, as they will perish in the absence of its smell.

Myth as *On Special!*, as *Ladies Night Discount!*
Myth as embedded in our mouths.

ᔓ

WHEN FORTUNE ALIGHTS ON US LIKE CROW to carrion, I wonder if we're compelled to fuck it up by making, prematurely, myth of it. Saying things like *blessed* or *God* or *meant to be* or *not meant to be.* I wonder if Harvey, in 1874, used, if only in his head, any of these words; if he thought of these words as a commodity; if he hoarded them, and felt rich; if Sarah Harvey, back home, the icy Newfoundland sea air creeping in through the walls, used any of these words; if Lloyd Hollett felt he was anointed with divine vision, the task of leashing insect to ice cream—anything to sell his obsessions to prospective buyers. Maybe Poppa Dave, in his last moments of life, in some hospital I never saw on Long Island, said something about fortune, or the other, earlier Moses, or rhinoceri, or ice cream, or the stock market. Perhaps he muttered something about decades' worth of love and sex and suppers with an orange-headed hunchback, about decades' worth of buying her the sort of flea-market perfume that would compel me, years later, to make myth of its awful smell; or maybe he was trapped, for those final few moments, in that Catskill Mountain resort ballroom in his early twenties, wailing into his saxophone, crystal chandeliers leaking their gauzy orange light over the white tablecloths, the circular tables, the plum napkins, and my grandma Ruth, then simply Ruth, walking into that room in her final teenage year, with her father on one arm, her mother on the other, white-gloved to the elbows, evening-gowned in black, her hair back then darker than her dress. I wonder if he, breathing his final breaths, imagined them being breathed into that saxophone of his youth as he declared, dumbstruck by the beautiful young Ruthie, expressing it only as a D note, if only in his head, *That's the girl I'm going to marry.* Surely he exhaled, some respirator or monitor wheezing or beeping away in the corner of the hospital room, the orange-headed Ruthie weeping her final *I love yous,* her final *I'm sorrys*, and remembered the courage it took to haul his short, fat body from behind his saxophone during the band's break, and woo the black-haired Ruthie away from her parents, to fall mutually, and quickly in love. I wonder how much of this story I have to sell myself until it becomes legendary.

൬

4,800,000,000,000 plates of squid, every year . . .

~

AT LEAST WE DON'T HAVE TO WONDER ABOUT the things we think we know. We think we know this:

In Conception Bay in the 1870s, "Eels are plentiful," "Sturgeons are rarely taken," "Lobsters are most abundant," "Oysters are not found," "Crabs are plentiful," "A few other species are met with, such as the pipe-fish, frog-fish, bellows-fish, sculpins, lance, cat-fish, and lump-fish," "Sharks are not uncommon."

We know that it was common practice for fishermen, such as Tommy Picco, Theophilus Picco, and Daniel Squires, "to land on the islands where [auks] bred, and fill their boats with the plump unwieldy birds (which on land could make no effort to escape), driving them . . . on board by the hundreds, or knocking them on the head with sticks. They feasted on the eggs," and sold their bones to the superstitious and the spiritual, "and even burned their bodies for fuel, in order to warm water to pick off the feathers, which were valuable."

In the nearby town of Bonavista (whose present-day Chamber of Commerce lists among the town's attractions a circular cliff-opening nicknamed the Dungeon, a Carriage Gun on the courthouse lawn, an eighteenth-century public torture site "where lawless people were punished as an example to others" affectionately nicknamed the

Whipping Post, and Atlantic puffins), "merchants... were in the habit of salting [auks] and selling them, in the winter season, instead of pork..."

The fishermen, "after slaughtering them ... sometimes shut them up in stone enclosures, in order to have them ready when wanted." Reverend Moses Harvey felt that "it is not wonderful that, under such circumstances, the great auk has been completely exterminated."

In scholar Weldon Thornton's annotated *Allusions in Ulysses*, the author wonders if, in regard to the source text's line, *Auk's egg, prize of their fray,* the auk indeed "has any special mythological or symbolic meaning" or if its usage is "to represent something exceedingly rare." The eleventh edition of the *Encyclopaedia Britannica* provides a soft, wishy-washy answer of sorts, declaring "A special interest attaches to the great auk (*Alca impennis*), owing to its recent extinction, and the value of its eggs to collectors."

Natural mythologist Héctor T. Arita romanticizes the great auk (or, as he writes, the Great Auk) in the "Extinction Gallery" section of his work *Mitología Natural.*

Author Errol Fuller, in his book *Extinct Birds,* writes about the great auk that, in Harvey's time, "the species in question had become so rare that to those who dwelt close to the rocky stacks and cliffs that line the shores of the North Atlantic, it was little more than a myth passed on here and there in folktale and legend."

Harvey believed the great auk to be "the connecting link between the fish and the bird, partaking of the nature of both," with its short wings, resembling "the fins of a fish."

W. Kitchen Parker, in his 1890 article "On the Morphology of the Duck and the Auk Tribes," deduces that, if the auk "is, indeed, the child of the reptile, it must forget its father's house; it must proceed beyond its progenitor. But if we are willing to see the bird's wing grow . . . in an unsettled state, ready for transformation into the higher type of limb, then the [evolutionary] difficulty is solved. It was a fish paddle; it was not to become a fore-foot; it did change into the framework of a bird's wing; in that respect, it is a perfect thing; as a paw, it is an abortion." Kitchen Parker goes on to say that his own description of this "beautiful metamorphosis" is scientifically sufficient, but in regards to the auk's "peculiarly fascinating" mythological implications, he is at a loss for words; to this aspect of the auk, "in a brief notice, it would be impossible to do proper justice."

And so, Kitchen Parker, in his nod to his own descriptive insufficiency, further mythologizes the bird. Parker points out that we often mythologize what we insufficiently understand, what we can't nail down with our limited linguistic tools. We forget our "father's house," and so we have our small adventures. And so we tell stories, make our sales pitches. We also tell stories about the things we have driven to extinction, or the things that so deftly (except in rare cases—things like the giant squid) escape our capture. We mythologize the things we have so completely killed. And we mythologize and commodify the things that, try as we might, we can't completely kill.

ᔓ

And: "A live giant squid is much desired."
The beak as pouty lips.
The body as Croatoan.

ᔓ

. . . WHICH THE SUPERSTITIOUS HERE, AND which the spiritual? Where is the context that allows us to easily define, determine . . . ? And how can we make a thirty-second commercial of it?

ᔓ

AMBERGRIS, THE WAXY, MATTE-GRAY, FLAMMAble sludge that the more intrepid of our marine biologists have extracted from the digestive systems of sperm whales, or have unearthed from pools of their beachy, terrestrial vomit, reeks of feces, reeks of musk and rubbing alcohol, and reeks (as the optimist capitalists would have us believe) like a cup of reduced dark roast coffee larded with far too much sugar. It is because naturalists have found a disproportionate number of giant squid beaks embedded into lumps of ambergris that we've deduced that the stuff is used, anatomically, to ease the passage of such unwieldy objects, objects that don't easily break down; objects that were once the sharp mouths of other, perhaps grander, beasts. It wasn't long after ambergris's discovery that we first starting using it, commonly, and in small amounts, in the sort of expensive perfumes that my grandmother's flea-market budget prevented her from ever spritzing onto her neck in order to seduce Poppa Dave. *Perfumiers* found that the sperm whale sludge/giant squid beak concoction helped to stymie the rate of evaporation in the perfume. It kept the perfume around just a little bit longer, so we could wear it, smell it, secure our lovers for that crucial extra time, after lesser perfumes had extinguished themselves.

Recently, trendy cocktail bars have begun adding ambergris to their avant-garde tonics. In Chicago, for instance, the bar Billy Sunday peddles the generically named "Cocktail"–a mixture of malted rye, Spanish brandy, palm sugar, water, North Bay bitters, and ambergris. Though the drink itself tasted like many others I've had, it is this latter ingredient (though I couldn't pick its flavor from the rest) that makes it memorable, compels me to pass on its story.

~

WE MYTHOLOGIZE AND WE EROTICIZE. THERE'S money in both . . .

Giant-Squid Erotica (to be read aloud to a lover): italicized sections taken from Professor Richard Owen's 1880 descriptions of some new and rare Cephalopoda in which he tries, Dear Readers, he tries to maintain a professional scientific distance from his material, but a throbbing excitement soon gets the better of him as he details his "*larger naked Cephalopods . . .*"

> *All the suckers are sessile. The mantle, or body-tunic,* swells *into a narrow fold,* a "*velum,*" *its corona. They round the hinder end of the body, meet, coalesce, and extend beyond that part, o'.* We draw each other into that *intervening recess* where we can become likewise *narrow and numerous.* We are *oblong, blind, conical,* suspending ourselves on *ganglion; the long diameter . . . The outer circular lip has its attachment to the bases of the arms strengthened, as in Loligopsis, by narrow muscular ridges or fraena, continued at one end upon the inner side of the base, ending in a point, and at the other end extend to the apex of the triangular process of the outer lip. These labial processes are not acetabuliferous. The two inner lips, answering, are present.* We are *struck by the spines of the horny rim of the suckers,*

enveloped by the webs, prey. We see something superadded, air-breathing, as it *envelops the struggling wasp or blue-bottle in a rapidly outspun web.* Call me "*uncus.*" I will call you "*ala.*" We will call our *muscular parts* to be *thickest at their widest parts, near the entry. Its apex is inserted into the middle, the cup, the homologous hoop or partial horny lining of the sucking-cup, fleshy vacuum into which it sinks.* Oh, *uncus Ignazio,* speak to me in Italian: "*oltre alla Seppia officinale si ritrovano nel mare... di gran mole... o siano i due lunghi tentacoli armati da un doppio ordine di artigli... Questa specie è di un gusto delicato...*" Yes. Good. Good. This is our "*unguiculata*" *proposition.* And I will speak to you in French, *On ne connaît de cette espèce qu'une partie d'un bras sessile gigantesque, couvert de crochets sur toute sa longueur. Je dois à l'obligeance de un beau dessin de ce bras déposé...* And *the cups gradually increase in size. From this aperture slightly projects the marin of the broad chitinous hoop lining the walls. The opposite surface of the fold has the paler tint, doubtless greater when the pigment was in lively motion along the free surface.* This is *the "Transit of Venus"* (which, it must be said, is the actual name of a nineteenth-century French expedition to find the giant squid).

∾

GIANT-SQUID VULGARITY (TO BE FORGOTTEN AS soon as it's read), by Ern Maunder, writer for the *Atlantic Guardian* in 1952:

> "Most self-respecting squids make a good handful and no more . . . The one above was captured late in December, 1933, at Dildo."

And, by Nancy Frost, affiliate of the British Museum of Natural History, "It is worthy to note that, of the two recent Newfoundland specimens, that from Harbour Main is a female, whilst that from Dildo was a male."

ᘓ

THE MYTH BEHIND THE NAMING OF THE BASQUE whaling station is drenched in whale blood. In the eviscerated bellies of the countless sperms and humpbacks from which the residents made their livelihood, heaps of semidigested giant squid crumbs were poured into the ocean, recycled as bait. Originally, the story goes that the whalers named their town Bilbao, but those antiwhaling Newfoundlanders changed the name as castigation for the bloodletting. "Men has died trying to get back to Dildo," says one local ex-whaler, "in the wars and in the boats. So the name stays."

൴

WHAT'S IN A NAME? TOURIST DOLLARS, APPARently. Each year, hundreds, if not thousands, of tourists flock to Dildo in order to purchase CAPTAIN DILDO baseball caps, DILDO HEAD coffee mugs, I SURVIVED DILDO DAY beer-can cozies, and, in spite of a history steeped in whale blood, DILDO: A HAPPY PLACE t-shirts.

൴

AND SO THERE'S HARVEY IN 1874, SENSING SOME animate eroticism in his chest, swelling dangerously close to vulgarity; maybe he senses some impending death, a return to some ill-named home. There's an electricity, certainly, the sense that something unforeseen is about to be bought, and therefore, sold. He watches the fishermen surround the fallen beast like so many scattered searchlights, smells that mineshaft-dark smell. There's Harvey excited, impulsive. There's Harvey exhaling, his breath tumbling into the air toward the giant squid. There's his heart opening like a wallet. There's Harvey trying, like Kitchen Parker, to come up with the words to describe what he sees, thinks, smells, feels. And there's Harvey, finding only these at his disposal: "A very great interest was awakened among naturalists . . . by an announcement which one of the present writers (Mr. Harvey) was fortunate enough to be able to make, of the discovery of a new species of cuttle-fish, of gigantic size, in the waters around Newfoundland."

Perhaps Harvey feared that the fishermen, burdened by their commercial values, would begin slicing the beast into small chunks, packaging it for sale as bait. Marine naturalists have often heaped scorn on fishermen for eating or feeding to their dogs what they themselves would have considered golden. In an 1872 letter regarding the capture by fishermen of a giant squid in the Grand Banks, Harvard professor Nathaniel Shaler, a former student of famed Swiss ichthyologist Jean Louis Agassiz, condescendingly wrote, "They [the fishermen] cut up one-half to bait their trawls, and caught with it one-hundred quintals of fish. The skeleton might have been brought in as well as not; but sailor-like, they did not think of it."

Shaler was also a white supremacist who only gradually relinquished his creationist ideals when he realized that he could manipulate Darwinism in order to support polygenism and peddle his own breed of racial discrimination to a wider audience. Shaler is most infamous for writing the article "The Negro Problem," published in the *Atlantic Monthly* in 1884, in which he professed that freed slaves were akin to "children lost in the wood, needing the old protection of the strong mastering hand" against their own "animal nature." Later in his career, he became Harvard's Dean of Sciences and was routinely voted Most Popular Teacher by the student body.

ᔓ

ANIMAL NATURE ASSERTS ITSELF. I'M AGAIN standing on the threshold of Moses Harvey's house, and those two old men are drinking from newer paper bags in the garage across the street. All around me, it seems, louder even than the coming-in ships blaring their foghorns, are wingbeats: How the sounds of some birds evoke an illusion of peace, others an illusion of menace. How the sounds of all birds fool us, commune with the sounds of the insects in some romantic linguistic. How I'm convinced that this doorbell I'm about to ring again is rigged to electrocute. Down the hill, another foghorn mourns another shipwreck, and I press the black button, but hear no ringing inside.

The heavy mail slot has been pushed closed in the only way it can be—from the inside. My contact information had been days-ago discovered, and ignored. I must come up with a new sales pitch. I must redesign myself to seduce, and maybe even dupe, my audience. I finger the purloined snake of paint in my windbreaker pocket. It's growing pliable. It begins to drizzle. Behind me, the sound of glass breaking, one of the old men dropping his bottle. Around the corner, on Temperance Street, an old woman in sealskin boots spits tobacco to the asphalt. In the Old Lower Battery, aged fishing stages take the rain into their porous stilts, just–as they have for years–resist collapsing. No one answers the door. Everywhere, tragedy. Commerce. Wings confusing themselves for other wings.

∾

HARVEY STOOD CONFUSED, SHIVERING BEFORE the water, fear and arousal spiraling in his heart, the beast that he believed he saw heaving, the pencil-lead sky, the "sailor-like" fishermen in orange, shuffling his brain like so many cards, the jacks and numbers, back to front, lit with indecency, recalling, conceivably, the night he stayed awake, sweating, though the sea air was downright cool, reading aloud to Sarah, in bed by yellow lantern light, Victor Hugo's *Toilers of the Sea*. We can assume that Harvey hugged himself, his body confused between an act of affection and an act of physical warming, confused about whether there was any significant difference between the two, and remembered Hugo's language, Hugo's own act of naming a then-thought-to-be-merely-fictional (though no less mythological) giant squid "the devil-fish."

Harvey used Hugo's word to describe what he was seeing, the sheer mass and glisten and penetrating stink, perhaps sulfuric, innately rooted to the chilly fear mechanisms that channel from the bases of our spines to the napes of our necks, damn near biblical, so much so that the only way to name the myth made flesh before him was to associate it with another myth, one that we'd previously been sold: that of the devil. Strange then, that both Harvey the naturalist and Harvey the reverend found the beast to be wholly holy, as opposed to wholly evil, which makes me wonder if Harvey, standing there on the shores of nineteenth-century Conception, was also confused about whether there was any significant difference between *these* two distinctions, or if both, like our drive to myth-make, were really just human invention, survival tactic, the instinct to exchange one thing for another, akin to what Joan Didion famously decided when she wrote, "We tell ourselves stories in order to live."

∾

THOUGH STILL I SPECULATE WHAT HARVEY TOLD himself (and what Lloyd Hollett still tells himself, and what the fuck Poppa Dave told Ruthie during the band's break in order to seduce her and seduce her *for life*), I know that Harvey told us this, revealing very little of his own personal, reverent truth: ". . . the reality surpassed [Hugo's] fiction." This actual giant squid was the car that, in spite of the salesman Hugo's effusive pitch, really *was* cherry, really *was* the car for Harvey.

And the reality also surpassed accounts (which at the time were dismissed as fictions "shrouded in a tissue of fable and exaggeration") of Aristotle and Pliny and Aelian and Strabo and Melville, who all, in their writings, believed that the Mediterranean waters were occupied by enormous, immeasurable cephalopods ("the most wonderful phenomenon of the secret seas," Melville wrote), claims which spawned the "squid-as-fad" concept in places like Paris, where, for a time, squid hats were in fashion and squid parties were the favored after-hours choice of the high society.

The reality surpassed the claims of Frank W. Lane, "the eminently successful popularizer of natural science," who believes that references to the giant squid appeared as early as 700 B.C.; that Homer's Scylla (Odysseus's antagonist) was no less than a giant squid, as Homer described the "six long sinuous necks outstretching before her," which is either a testament to Homer's obsession with marine mythology, or his lifelong love affair with a primitive version of linguini.

Harvey's reality surpassed the fiction, or at least the romantic flights of fancy, of W. Saville-Kent, a "sometime assistant in the Natural History department of the British Museum and late Superintending Naturalist to the Brighton Aquarium" who wrote in April 1874 of the giant squid, or his conception of it, "... no kingdom in fairyland was ever invested with such a wealth of form and beauty . . . No gem-laden forest of the 'Arabian Nights' ever grew such wondrous living crystal trees . . . No fairy banquet table was ever bedecked with ornaments of so chaste and rare design as might be borrowed from the exhaustless store of exquisitely carved vases, sheaths, or bucklers, which shelter from extinction the slender spark of mystic life as it exists in Nature's . . . forms," a description which evokes, in both exoticism and prudence, sex with an overseas chastity belt.

Harvey's "reality" conversed, across time and ocean, with that of the unnamed Japanese sculptor who made one of the first carvings of a giant squid attacking a person. Of this sculpture, Frank Buckland, of the *Fellows of the Zoological Society of London*, writes in *Land and Water*: "This carving is an inch and a half long, and about as big as a walnut. The unfortunate lady has been seized [by the squid] while bathing. One extended arm [is] coiling round the lady's neck. The other arms . . . are twined round, grasping the lady's body and waist. The colour of the body of the creature, together with the formidable aspect of the eye, are wonderfully represented," a description which, gender-confused, evokes the Venus of Willendorf in distress, her story silkscreened onto something the size of a testicle. One wonders here about the emasculation of the savior, the power of the damsel to inhabit the vas deferens, the knight in shining armor small-dicked and kicked in the balls, the squid as blockage to the sperm. One wonders at which level of bullshit exists the description lent to the carving by countless collectors and curators, who couldn't wait to once again tighten their lips, engage the plosive–blocking the vocal tract so that all airflow briefly ceases, the thin giddiness of asphyxiation briefly ticking the brain–begin pronouncing the long-rehearsed word "priceless."

Harvey's "reality" communicated with that of Carolus Linnaeus, godfather of binomial nomenclature, who, in 1735, published the first edition of his masterwork *Systema Naturae*, which set about classifying and naming all things in nature, and which included, amazingly, the kraken, under the moniker *Sepia microcosmos*. (This was about 120 years before the Danish zoologist and spectacularly named Johannes Japetus Smith Steenstrup dared make a similar assertion, and lent the mythological kraken the language of science, claiming it existed and was a cephalopod).

Linnaeus's entry was removed by the time the second edition went to press, and Linnaeus was ridiculed as gullible for having included it in the first place, for being seduced by "the mere fabrications of a distorted mind." His critics and colleagues, metaphorically kicking him in his metaphorical balls, similarly gave him shit for naming the banana, *Musa paradisiaca*, claiming that, according to essayist Karen Hays, "he believed its yellow fingers grew from the Tree of Knowledge, whose forbidden fruit (though so often seedless) appealed to our species in order to propagate its own." By the time the scientific community got its hands on Linnaeus's second edition, the godfather of binomial nomenclature had taken a job teaching botany at Uppsala University, and the giant squid, having been given its brief and small entry into reality in 1735, once again retreated to the realm of myth.

I wonder if, a full 130 years after Linnaeus cited the beast, when a piece of giant squid tentacle was obtained by the French steamship *Alecton* (a name borrowed from a genus of firefly beetle that Linnaeus was successful in categorizing), Arthur Mangin, French zoologist, shook his fists in the air as he bellowed that it wasn't a tentacle at all, but only "the remains of a sea plant!" and urged, fearfully, "the wise, and especially the man of science, not to admit into the catalogue those stories which mention extraordinary creatures... the existence of which would be... a contradiction of the great laws of harmony and equilibrium which have sovereign rule over living nature."

We can only ask if nature really was harmonious and balanced back then, or if this is just another ad slogan, jingle.

And we can only hope, a full 150 years after Linnaeus cited the beast, and a full decade after Harvey photographed it, that Henry Lee, occasional naturalist of the Brighton Aquarium, knew he was chained to an archaic, sad argument when he dismissed, in *Sea Fables Explained,* the giant squid as "a boorish exaggeration, a legend of ignorance, superstition, and wonder."

And Thomas Helm (author of *Shark!*), in 1962, felt his heart accelerate as he wrote, "Those who continue to doubt that the sea contains monsters simply have not seen the giant squid."

And Peter Benchley, of *Jaws* fame, felt boyish again when, in his book *The Beast* he wrote–in a shamelessly *Boys' Life*-y tone–that the giant squid "killed without need, as if Nature, in a fit of perverse malevolence, had programmed it to that end."

ᔓ

AND HARVEY RETREATED INTO HIS JACKET, HIS hands shaking in the wind, and heard the waves crashing against the giant squid's body, a sound more hollow than that of a wave crashing onto earth. Did he think of Ireland or of Sarah, or of God? Did he think of voicelessness? Or did he think only of what he saw, a creature whose longest arm measured over twenty-four feet ("Hugo's devil-fish was only four or five feet between the extremities of the outspread arms"), "and between their outspread extremities were fifty-two feet?" He surely remembered last

October 26, when Tommy Picco, Theophilus Picco, and Daniel Squires interrupted his potato meal with their gift of tentacle. Certainly, he recalled their own stories, and reimagined their ordeal. It was October and, given average October temperatures for the area, 34 degrees Fahrenheit. Colder on the water.

Tommy, Theophilus, and Daniel had been out rocking in a small boat, gathering nausea in spite of their experience off the eastern flank of Conception Bay's Belle Isle. "Observing something floating in the water," Harvey writes, "they rowed up to it and one of them struck it with his boat-hook." The men (who Harvey rarely calls by their names in his written accounts, save for Little Tommy) jumped back toward the boat's center, and one of them, the largest of the men (this would have been either Theophilus Picco or Daniel Squires), fell down. He felt something rise in his chest, burn in his throat. He felt the chill stab at the innermost points of his ears and he felt like running on water. "Instantly," Harvey writes, "the mass showed that it was animated by putting itself into motion." The smallest of the men (this would have been twelve-year-old Tommy Picco), dropped whatever he was holding–a thermos of coffee, a harpoon, his other hand, his genitals, no matter–and turned to run and found he was on a small rowboat, and tripped over the largest of the men who was struggling to his feet, and

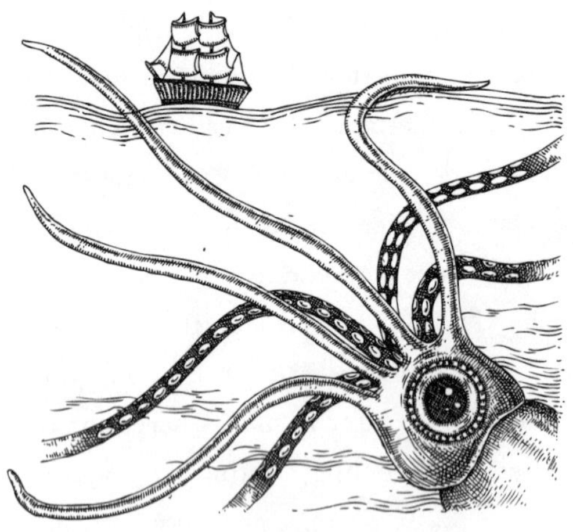

uttered the nineteenth-century Newfoundland equivalent of "Oooohhhhh, shiiiiit . . ."

"A huge beak reared itself from among the folds," Harvey says, "and struck the boat."

Now, on the shore in 1874, Harvey approached the fishermen. He may have confused them for Tommy, Theophilus and Daniel. They did not look up at him, fear-spittle still holding to their cold lips, hands still shaking, and Harvey, hands also shaking, asked for their story, as I ask in vain for his.

About the 1873 trio, Harvey tells me what they told him–sells it to me–that what happened next was that, as the men struggled to their feet and looked around the tiny boat for their mothers, the Devil-fish stared at them with its giant eyes, "glared at them ferociously," would not, under any circumstances, look away first. "Petrified with fear," one man threw up on his rubber boots, and the orange rubber jacket-back of his mate, "but before they had time" to snatch up their oars and attempt a feeble "escape, two corpse-like arms shot out from around the head and flung themselves across the boat."

"From that corpse-like embrace, there is no escape."

Harvey's prose here makes it unclear as to whether the giant squid grabbed the men and flung them across the boat, or if the men themselves, out of some primitive fear launched their own bodies across the boat to escape the squid's "embrace," or if the men were telling "stories in order to live," or if Harvey was, or if I am.

The arms were both "corpse-like" and "animated," and Harvey knew that this was paradox, and Harvey knew that this was story, and Harvey knew, in hindsight, what the men surely felt instinctively at the time, that "had those slimy arms with their powerful suckers, once attached themselves to the boat, it would speedily have been drawn under the water and its occupants would have been brought within reach of the monster's powerful beak."

That Harvey lent the beast, for which he had obvious reverence or (as Sarah Harvey might have put it) unhealthy obsession, terms like "devil" and "monster," may point to our need to mythologize and study and spin tales about that which we fear. We are obsessed with the things we simultaneously (at least linguistically, in Harvey's case) demonize; and we will talk and talk and write and write, ever-pitching, until others begin to show signs of sharing our obsessions. It takes one man to demonize; it takes a village of demonizers to make a myth.

In response to this notion, to Harvey's diction choices, to questions like, So why the giant squid, after all? we have to ask other questions. How did this particular beast become the basis for our kraken (a beast "invented" and so-named in the sixteenth century by Olaus Magnus, Archbishop of Uppsala [where Linnaeus later taught], after listening to the tales of Norwegian fishermen), a legend which, according to Kent, "only rendered previous confusion worse confounded, and hid behind a yet more impenetrable veil of mystery that line of demarkation between truth and fiction which doubtless existed at the outset?" The word *kraken* translates as "uprooted tree," a name Magnus justifies in believing that "their Forms are horrible, their Heads Square . . . and they have sharp and long horns round about, like a Tree rooted up by the Roots." This explanation does nothing, of course, to lift the "veil of mystery," or explain why we associate the proverbial Sea Monster with an image of the giant squid, if not a stunted tree.

Dr. Clyde Roper states, "My strong belief (and observation) is that people must have their monsters, a human trait that begins in childhood and perseveres throughout adulthood ('tho [*sic*] you would find deniers who refuse to recognize their monsters . . . or to let on they have them . . .). Even little kids display that innate need . . . long before they have a clue what a dinosaur actually was/is, and in spite of (or because of!) the fact that they could be huge and have very big teeth."

And so, in regards to this definition of our need for monstrosity, and how notions of fortune (*When fortune alights on us like crow to carrion . . .*) revise and confuse and redraft themselves when embedded in this need, Harvey continues to tell his story of the fishermen's story, allowing us, as audience, an odd, but not altogether comfortable sigh of relief (see: the killing of Osama Bin Laden, one of our contemporary krakens, about whom various narratives spin) as "One of the men, however, had the presence of mind to seize a small hatchet that fortunately [*fortunately*] lay in the bottom of the boat, and with a couple of blows he severed the arms as they lay over the gunwale of the boat. The creature uttered no cry of pain; but at once moved off from the boat and ejected an enormous quantity of inky fluid, which darkened the water for two or three hundred yards."

We don't know how the men, and in turn Harvey,

measured the spread of the defensive ink. We can't know if any of them privately associated this ejecta with ejaculation. We can never be privy to the elusive "whole story," as it's ever usurped by legend. How else would any of the world's cultures whose tenets are so dependent on generationally passed-on legends live? Without legends inherited and exchanged among us like so many goods and services, without story, upon what would they, and we, base their/our values, religions, laws, ethics, logic, emotions? If the so-called Devil-fish cried out in pain when that fisherman chopped his or her legs off, thereby identifying with us humans, would we have had that "innate need" as Dr. Roper calls it, to make a myth of it?

ᘏ

SAYS KANALOA, THE POLYNESIAN GOD OF THE ocean (represented via totem as a giant squid), loosely translated, *Here, in these depths, even the Rapture is a commodity.*

Part Three

ALL OF THESE SUCKERS

“SOMEONE’S EXPERIENCE OF PAIN,” GILBERT LEWIS of the University of Cambridge’s Department of Social Anthropology writes, “cannot be shared . . . by another. The experience is private. Yet in ordinary life . . . we often try to appreciate the quality or intensity of someone else’s pain.

“Given the privacy of pain, the sufferer must express it to make it known. . . . Darwin remarked that animals which are normally mute, like the hare, . . . scream in extreme pain . . . But Darwin also noted that some animals seem to suffer . . . pain soundlessly–for instance the horse with a broken leg, silent, trembling, runneled with sweat.

“With man . . . there is a voluntary element in response . . .

The ways to convey this information or to gain sympathy are subject to particular conventions . . ."

Without expression, or at least expression that conforms to the contextual conventions we understand, there is no sympathy. There is only the other, the monster, the cautionary tale, the story. In the Western world, expressions of sympathy, the desire to comfort, to ease pain, are often made manifest in a collection of physical, usually gifted, objects. Two of the more popular are flowers (obviously), and ice cream. Habitual cravings for ice cream are called, by some psychologists, "sympathy cravings." It's a balm for pain, whether physical or emotional, but, as Lewis stresses, "the sufferer must express it." And so, such notions trickle casually, but importantly, into our language. Like the gut-shot hare, we must scream. I scream. You scream. We all scream.

Tonsils, cheating lover, miscarriage, loneliness, giant squid carcasses "washed ashore dead or dying on lonely beaches or in isolated coves following autumn storms . . ." We need salve, just as Lloyd Hollett needs to console that poor kid, bravely holding his bladder while bravely holding that emperor scorpion, with a double scoop of mint chocolate chip. Ice cream is Hollett's condolence card to the visitors whose passion for insects does not match his own. Ice cream is not only his expression of sympathy to such folks, but also of connection. *In spite of my love for*

bugs, and what you may perceive (as so many have before you) as my weirdness, I am human like you. It is his own salve against loneliness, one that allows him to express his unique passions while still, however tenuously, connecting to the masses. It is mutual reassurance. Poppa Dave was likely right in spite of his own obesity and diabetic journey: *there's always room for it.*

BUT THE SQUID OFFERED THOSE THREE FRIGHTened fishermen no screams. All they heard were their own. Even though they retained their legs and their lives, their sympathies lay with themselves, if only because they expressed their fear and pain verbally, according to our "particular conventions." These fishermen further mistook the squid's ink for blood—black blood—further stressing the Other, the Monster, the Myth . . . It is not like us. If it does not scream when dismembered, if it bleeds black, it can't be.

ᘓ

THE REGENERATION OF LOST ARMS DOES NOT occur in the giant squid.

ᘓ

IN A 2003 *DISCOVER* MAGAZINE ARTICLE, "SQUID Sensitivity," Stanford University Professor of Biology and Electrophysiologist (one who studies the wiring of the nervous system) William F. Gilly "considers whether or not a squid feels pain" as we can define it. Detailing an expedition to capture squid for study, the article engages

> a couple of the squid, too ripped up to release . . . One, lying in the inky bilge, seems to have set its eyes on Gilly. The creature is dying, its color fading, its electricity ebbing. Air rasps through its siphon. Overtaken by what he later describes as a "profound sadness" that "must have been lying latent for 25 years," Gilly pulls out his knife, bends between the thwarts, and puts the squid out of its misery.

> "Before then I never felt small—by that I mean diminished—in sacrificing such animals for scientific work," he recalls. "Maybe it was the size of the eye—it made it seem more living."

He cited an earlier account of a giant squid dying on the southern shore of Trinity Bay, Newfoundland: "Its power was gone, and in a few moments, the creature that had been all that was typical of power and strength became a soft, yielding mass of flesh."

ᔓ

TO EASE HIS "PROFOUND SADNESS," I WANT GILLY to have comforted himself with some of the best ice cream in Baja California at Tepoznieves. Tepoznieves is, itself, named after a myth, that of the Aztec god Tepoztecatl, patron saint of the sacred alcoholic pulque, to whom the wind god dedicated a special ice cream, the edible medium through which Tepoztecatl, and then in turn demigods, and then in turn humans, could speak with the wind. The parlor is famous for such flavors as Mahona (rose petal, two types of chocolate, raisins, and almonds), Thousand Flowers [doubly comforting] (cream, almonds, and herbal tea), and Poblana (coffee, sweet potato, and Bailey's Irish Cream), and for the vegetally minded, lettuce ice cream, celery ice cream, carrot, avocado, cactus . . . flavors that never graced the ice-cream truck I drove around Chicago during that awful heat wave, the poor of Chicago mythologized, other beasts who can somehow (but somehow did not) survive extreme weather without air conditioning or heat, left to die, their legacy an excretion of inky fluid that stained the back pages of the Chicago newspapers for a couple of days, and then disappeared.

ᘓ

HARVEY WRITES OF THE GIANT SQUID, AFTER Tommy Picco chopped its arm off: "Most likely, it retired into the depths of the ocean to die alone, otherwise it would have been attacked and devoured by its fellows. Sympathy among Devil-fish could hardly be looked for."

ᘓ

IN HIS SOLITUDE TRAVELING THROUGH NEWfoundland, as salve against loneliness perhaps, author John Gimlette writes, "Whenever I came upon an outport, tucked in its cove, I bought an ice-cream." I wonder if he ran into Lloyd Hollett.

ᘓ

HARVEY WRITES, "MAN IS A BORN EXPLORER. His first migration from the Garden of Eden has been followed by countless and ever-widening waves of human population, flowing around the globe, and occupying its solitudes . . . What were life, divested of all its poetry and romance?"

࿀

DESPITE MY KEEN STALKING CAPABILITIES, I'VE yet to make contact with the Harvey house's current resident. As usual, I drown failure with food. The androgynous waitress at Bacalao restaurant is working the dinner shift tonight, and I start with cocktails—the Berrypicker: Iceberg Vodka, lime cordial, vermouth, and partridgeberry syrup; the Out of the Bog: Iceberg Gin, Galliano, and bakeapple tincture. Poetry and romance . . . Maybe a little pain, too. I tell her about my unrequited affair with the old Harvey doorstep, about my gearing up for a nighttime doorbell ring, my trying of a different hour, about my getting desperate, about my having traveled such a long way . . . About how this born explorer thing is overstatement at best, bullshit at worst. She stares at my drained second cocktail—still preappetizer—and nods patiently.

Soon, I fortify myself with variations on food I've already eaten here: salt cod and potato fritters with garlic aioli, and caribou medallions with partridgeberry sauce, gnocchi flavored with Newfoundland savory, and gelled Rodrigues Barrens Blend wine, so named for the swampy, mossy, predominantly uninhabitable mish that stretches throughout the province, lurking just beyond the confines of the settlements. I'm getting anxious. I skip dessert. I walk down the hill, and along George Street, a commercial stretch that Moses Harvey once called "a very eligible situation," and now offers eligibility of another kind: dive bar after dive bar, each with their own long lines of mostly fiftysomethings waiting to get in, boorish men carrying blow-up sex dolls, women baring their breasts at the giant policemen's backs, a pair of young buskers in nuns' habits playing banjo and accordion songs about marijuana, their sacramental cups balanced on the street curb, overflowing with Loonies. Bald bouncers preside over the entryways, their huge bodies doing their best to prevent the bad Mellencamp covers from commingling with the bad Rod Stewart covers coming from next door.

I duck into the one bar without a line, without signage. I stand at the thickly lacquered driftwood bar and do a shot of Screech rum, but, shirking tradition, don't kiss the cod. I can't tell one song from another. A young couple at the bar talks of a local obligation to Canadian film patronage, of culinary tourism, of a lack of fresh fish in Newfoundland, of industrial waste on stunning coastlines, of the benefits of running. The younger, tank-topped bartender says something to them that sounds like "spattered gas pumps soldiering lonely in the oatmeal gravel."

In this I sense a great metaphor, but can't quite capture it. I trace my fingers along the images and words carved into the bar's surface, as if trying to crack code–clumsy versions of genitalia, declarations of love *4ever*, hearts punctured by arrows, slogans and insults in both English and Gaelic; next to a carving of a stick figure in a dress: the word, *máthair*, which I know means *mother*, and next to the carving of a crude rectangular penis: the word, *ollmhór*, which I will later find out means *giant*.

Behind me, a table of seven sit in matching yellow all-weather jackets. They speak of a herd of buffalo, imported from Alberta, which, years ago outside the town of Fortune, committed mass suicide by jumping off of a cliff. "They were used to the flatlands," one says, "and couldn't handle all this feckin' landscape." No one at the table asks if any of the buffalo had screamed while falling, cried out as they hit the ground, crushed in that brief moment before dying.

The walls, though windowless, are lined with sallow curtains. The whole place, if the lights were turned up, would surely be revealed to be as depressing as a hospital cafeteria–the light coffee-colored, cigarette-stained, the whole place rusted, caulked, chipped, and a little grandmotherly. I wonder how I'm handling this landscape.

The place feels tenuous. Disconnected. Homeless. This whole place is a passing phase. Near the rear bathroom, old vending machines peddle forgotten retro vendibles—Skittles and Reese's Pieces and cans of Hawaiian Punch. Potbellied men and boys thrust against old cabinet video games—Sega Virtua Fighter 2 and Extreme Hunting and Atari San Francisco Rush 2049 and Sammy Faster Than Speed and Gottlieb/Capcom Street Fighter II: Champion Edition pinball (for which I can't locate a Loonie in my pocket), a dim drunken cornucopia of joysticks and steering wheels and plastic orange rifles on hoses.

Old women waiting to pee speak of new shipwrecks, speak of the subsequent deaths with the nonchalance of the gritty toothless for whom the ocean isn't pretty, but thoroughfare and factory. They laugh and do little waltzes and drain their plastic cups of their Sex on the Beaches. I do what I think Poppa Dave would have me do. I jump up. I listen for any kind of clue. I back to the door. I nod at the bartender. I wave my arms like this. I get out of here.

Up Ordnance Street, I trail a skinny man with thick glasses—white cap, no socks, carrying four canvas tote bags—toward the Harvey home, thinking this must be him, the current resident. My heart sinks when he turns into Zachary's Restaurant: BOLOGNA ON SPECIAL!

Back at Devon Row, the streets are mostly free of people; the sounds of the ships once again predominate. A knit mummer doll lies facedown in a brackish puddle, lit up yellow in the streetlight, recalling the dissipation of the old Newfoundland tradition of mummering: disguising oneself (the dolls represent this with a horrifying miniature potato sack cinched over the head—something of tiny shame or torture) at Christmas, and going from door to door putting on a little theatrical performance for the house's inhabitants. The hosts were obligated to ply the mummers with booze (as payment for the unsolicited performance), until they could guess the identity of the masked intruder. Now, the dolls swarm the souvenir shops, and now the doll simulates drowning in a rain puddle right in front of Moses Harvey's old house—all good traditions shrouding their original aggression in some faux-wistful all-in-good-fun-ism.

A boy throws up at the vertex of the Sheraton's U-shaped driveway. A doorman in red runs the length of the latus rectum barking, "Mop! Mop!"

Another boy cups his hands and tries to peer into the darkened window of the Wig Shop, hoping, perhaps, to steal a keen brunet monofilament for his cancerous mother. LeMoine's School bears a handwritten sign that says CLOSED UNTIL TOMORROW.

The alcohol helped, and helps. I walk right up the three steps and jab at the Harvey doorbell. I don't care if I wake anybody up. I prepare my performance. I hope it's as painless as possible.

ꟹ

SHIVERING SHORESIDE IN 1874, HARVEY REMEMbered, rehearsed, and later wrote about, what happened next regarding those three fishermen who, not quite a year earlier, interrupted his potato and laurel supper. After Tommy Picco anatomized the Devil-fish, "The men saw no more of it, and having dragged the amputated arms into the boat, made for shore. The shorter and thicker of the two arms was thrown carelessly aside and destroyed," which obviously pissed Harvey off, controlling himself as he wrote, trying not to call the Monster Killers stupid bumpkins, biting his Reverential tongue and opting to call them "careless" instead.

Later, as he wrote of their story and his reaction to it (referring to himself in the third person), he pined for that lost arm, speculating that it "was described as six feet in length and ten or twelve inches in circumference." Thank God, Harvey must have felt, that "the longer arm was brought to St. John's by the fishermen, and Mr. Harvey was fortunate enough to secure it." And it is precisely this fortune that allowed Harvey to extend and perpetuate the myth of the giant squid by, strangely enough, making it real, albeit a real monster. The fish birthed in Hell, whose salvaged leg "must have been thirty feet" and "broadened out like an oar and then tapered to a fine, tongue-like point," and "was thickly covered with suckers, having thorny, teethed edges, the largest of them over an inch in diameter, the smallest not larger than a split pea."

"All of these suckers," Harvey wrote, "acting together, would establish such a grasp on an object as it would be impossible to escape from. The fishermen described the body of the monster as being of immense size."

Can a beast capable of inflicting such pain actually feel pain too? Is this too much for us to grasp? Do such questions ruin his narrative agenda? If Harvey secured a piece of a "monster," wouldn't this allow him the opportunity for further self-aggrandizement?

Of his 1874 walk along the shore in the cold rain, of his coming upon what he later described as "a perfect specimen," long after shedding his wet clothes and, imaginably, whispering, with freezing lips, giddily into Sarah's ear, his rib cage brushing hers, and delivering a series of sermons–some of his last–engaging all manner of gods and monsters, Harvey would once again engage the intersection of fortune and myth, this time proving the existence of such an intersection via image: "Mr. Harvey had again the good fortune . . . to obtain possession of the animal. He had it measured and photographed. . . ."

∾

ONE MIGHT IMAGINE, AS I MAY, WHAT WOULD have happened to those connubial and complacent Romans at the end of Fellini's *La Dolce Vita* had that unblinking, net-trapped sea monster—that repulsive but all-too-real and all-too-dead Christ figure, one which predicts Marcello the protagonist's subsequent inability to communicate with just about anything—come back to life and, with sucker and mouth, stripped the human characters of both their complacency and their flesh. One might imagine the screams, and the inability of the monster, ever-silent, to empathize with such a horrified audible expression. One might imagine that, dead or alive, beautiful or ugly, all communication is destined to be miscommunicated. How, to a dog, our whispered affection sounds like a hurricane. How we salt the very snails whose concentric shells are the objects in nature that most closely resemble the ventricles of our strange human hearts.

∾

GILBERT LEWIS WONDERS IF WE CAN EVER REALLY empathize with another's pain, whether fellow human or animal. Even if we speak the same "language," we don't speak the same language. Something forever separates us. Or everything does. Sex and sexuality, economic class, age, body, region, religion, "values," shell, heart . . . The ways in which we eat, love, fuck, sleep, raise children, and regard the dead. And, the ways in which we regard pain itself.

Lewis mentions, "in 1832, the Mandan Indians of Missouri hoisted [the braves] [to swing] from rawhide thongs attached to skewers pierced through the flesh of their breast and backs, . . . from which they . . . dragged weights until they were torn free. Pain was chosen to test a man and prove him . . . [or perhaps a] person is expected to give outward signs of his grief . . . as though to match the inner feeling by a corresponding outer pain."

Either way, it seems an expression of pain, whether overt or implied, self-inflicted or not, for whatever reason, resides in our desperate and futile attempt to communicate to others our profoundly "private" experience which, try as we might, "cannot be shared."

ᘏ

ESSAYIST EULA BISS ASKS TO WHAT DEGREE WE self-identify via the pain—emotional, physical, social—we experience. "If no pain is possible, then another question—is no pain desirable? Does the absence of pain equal the absence of everything?"

And so, though we can never truly communicate—to the point of significant empathy—our pain to another, should we choose not to try, what then are we communicating? That we feel no pain? That we are more absent than another who makes the desperate and futile attempt? Are those who waste their breath seen as more *present* than those who choose silence? Does the giant squid, in its lack of vocal expression when Little Tommy Picco chopped its arms (or legs) off, render itself both giant and absent? And how can we humans, with our emotional, physical, and social languages, attempt to reconcile those two definitions? How can we who deem ourselves privileged enough to afford a place with heat and A/C reconcile both the guilt we feel in regard to those who can't, and the fear (that one day we may be forced to forfeit our own luxuries should those less fortunate be granted louder voice) that often accompanies that guilt? By dismissal perhaps. By easy labels. By *monster.* By *myth.*

ᔓ

BISS WRITES: "GRAB A CHICKEN BY ITS NECK or body—it squawks and flaps and pecks and threshes like mad. But grab a chicken by its feet and turn it upside down, and it just hangs there blinking in a waking trance. Zeroed. My mother and I once hung the chickens like this on the barn door for their necks to be slit. I like to imagine that a chicken at zero feels no pain."

And, "The [Wong-Baker] Pain Scale measures only the intensity of pain, not the duration."

And, "When I complained of pain as a child, my father would ask, 'What kind of pain?' "

And, "Assigning a value to my own pain has never ceased to feel like a political act. I am a citizen of a country that ranks our comfort above any other concern."

Is it possible even to associate pain with a number? Does *seven* accurately serve to communicate to others, or help define for ourselves, a headache, a broken heart, centuries of cultural oppression, any kind of dismemberment, the lack of A/C in a midwestern heatwave? Do we even speak our own language?

ᔓ

CAN I EVER KNOW MY GRANDFATHER IF I CAN never know his pain?

ᔓ

THE GIANT SQUID IS NOT YET KNOWABLE. THERE is no single source of information related to it "anywhere in the world. In order to read up on their specialty, cephalopod biologists have to sift through thousands of journals to find pertinent articles."

Here are the top six reasons, according to Clyde Roper,

why "no modern, comprehensive monographic treatment of the [giant squid] exists," and why our knowledge of the giant squid remains, even today, "in a chaotic state":

1. The Squid Diaspora: "very few complete, well preserved specimens exist and those that do are widely scattered around the world. . . . The whales know where they live, but we don't";
2. Mishandling of the Body: "most specimens are damaged, incomplete or in various stages of decomposition by the time a teuthologist examines them";
3. The Sum of Its Parts Equals Zero: "nominal species often are based just on parts or very incomplete, damaged specimens, so comparable characters are not described for each 'species' ";
4. The Inadequate Reservation: "facilities for long term preservation and storage of multiple specimens are rare to non-existent";
5. We Can't Understand What We're Saying: "literature is scattered in many languages and in disparate, often obscure journals";
6. In Repetition Is Salve: "in the early literature individual specimens often were reported many times by several different authors."

∾

WE KNOW MORE ABOUT THE DINOSAURS THAN we do about the giant squid. And we're getting desperate. French yachtsman Olivier de Kersauson spotted a giant mass in the middle of the Atlantic. It was nighttime, and there was no moon, and there were tentacles on his rudder longer than a city bus.

"It was enormous," he said. "I've been sailing for forty years and I've always had an answer for everything–for hurricanes and icebergs. But I didn't have an answer for this. It was terrifying."

New Zealand marine biologist Steve O'Shea is scrambling to answer these terrifying questions, and betting his family's savings on it. O'Shea is going deaf, and has no money left to buy a hearing aid. "If I don't find a giant squid soon," he says, "I'll be ruined."

O'Shea believes the giant squid, in spite of its lore, to be a delicate, gentle creature. "We have to move beyond this mythical monster and see it as it is," he says. "Isn't that enough?"

Roper himself–now seventy-four–after enduring a recent quadruple-bypass operation, promised his own family–his wife and two children and five grandchildren–that he would finally give up on the fundraising and subsequent squid expeditions, though he secretly divulges, "I'm hoping to make one more voyage."

The world of squid hunting is–to borrow a phrase

involving a different species—dog-eat-dog. Jean-Michel Cousteau—Jacques's kid—claims, "There's this all-out battle between these guys. [They] totally hate each other."

Roper says that he doesn't know of a giant-squid hunter who doesn't work in complete secrecy. But even of lesser species of squid, Roper says, "The only ones you catch are the slow, the sick, and the stupid."

O'Shea calls his fellow squid hunters "cannibals. These people are vicious. They want you to fail so they can be first."

The giant squid has a beak. The tyrannosaur has arched nasal bones, which kept it from decimating its own skull while crushing the skulls of its prey with a lower jaw capable of applying 200,000 newtons of force.

~

IN HIS BOOK, *EXOTIC ZOOLOGY*, WILLY LEY STATES that the giant squid's existence is one of the only things we know about them. A great section of this book is devoted to examining cryptozoology, literally "the study of hidden animals." The book's first section is entitled "Myth?" and examines the ways in which creatures of legend intersect with ones actual. In this section, he makes "almost-real" the unicorn, the sirrush, the Cyclops, relict dinosaurs, sea serpents, and the Yeti. Evolution from myth to reality and back, like actual evolution, is so slow we don't realize it's painful.

ᔓ

LEWIS STRESSES: "HURT TO THOSE WE DO NOT know concerns us less. Sympathy depends . . . on being able to identify imaginatively with someone else. We strike a tree without concern. We may hurt some creatures callously, yet the more we see them as . . . like ourselves (. . . pet dog) the less easy it becomes. What . . . differs among cultures . . . is the readiness to grant only some partial, or a fully equal humanity to other races, ethnic groups or classes . . . The morality which . . . governs the infliction of pain differs among cultures not so much in its basic premises as in the field of people whom it is held to apply to—a field that may be restricted to the few who come within one's own group or category of reference . . ."

Mark Zborowski, in the *Journal of Social Issues*, found that Eskimos begin to feel increasing heat as painful at a different level than an American, who feels it at a different level than a Nigerian; that, among those of European descent, Italians "tend to call for immediate relief of pain by any means, such as drugs;" that, Jewish-Americans demand relief from pain, but, due to a cultural skepticism and distrust of the future, they often continue to complain of the pain even after it has subsided; that "Old" or "Yankee" Americans have a higher tolerance for severe pain than do the Italians and Jews; that, in these studies, "the levels [of pain tolerance] were found to vary significantly depending on whether the person conducting the experiment was obviously someone like them–of Jewish background–or obviously of Yankee or Italian American extraction."

"Only a human being," Zborowski marvels, "may prefer starvation to the breaking of a religious dietary law . . ."

Should we choose physical pain over social (or religious) pain, does that make pain done to the body less painful than other types? To what degree are certain kinds of pain a cultural choice–which is really, as Lewis may stress, an individual, private choice?

~

In France, they say, *Aie!*
In New Guinea, they say, *Udei! Udjiao!*
In Japan, they say, *Itai!*
In Hindi, they say, *A'uca!*
In Afrikaans, they say, *Eina!*
In Latin, they say (or said), *Heu!*
In Arabic, they say, *Guoy-ha!*
In Azerbaijani, they say, *Uf!*

In Filipino, they say, *Aray!*
In Thailand, they say, *Xuy tay!*
In Turkey, they say, *Ooo!*
In Haitian Creole, they say, *Name!*
In the U.S., we say, *Ouch!*
The giant squid, of course, says nothing, merely lies
dying, its color fading...

ඉ

ON GOOGLE, WHEN TRYING TO UNCOVER VARious Native American expressions for *Ouch!*, the closest the search engine could come was listing a series of pages translating the word *Touch*.

ඉ

LLOYD HOLLETT BELIEVES BUTTERFLIES CAN ease our pain. In addition to ice cream and insects, Hollett is also fascinated with Near Death Experiences. "I am not sure where the interest came from," he says. "Maybe it is from a desire to know that there really is life after death, which takes away some of the fear of dying.

"Many people regard butterflies as symbols of rebirth. I also feel that if we have the power to move something after we die that a butterfly would be one of the easiest things to manipulate."

~

WHEN SWARMS OF MIGRATING MONARCH BUTterflies passed over Ohio on September 20, 1892–in the aftermath of the Great Fire that melted St. John's, Newfoundland–the residents of Cleveland mistook them for cholera germs. People shielded the faces of their babies. People slammed their windows. People ran in fear. People killed them with rolled-up newspaper. The butterflies who lived fled to Mexico, a sanctuary, where the residents there greeted them with reverence.

~

Even a pig can keep a conscience,
and kindness can touch his heart.

–Moses Harvey.

~

IN 1874, AS HARVEY CAME UPON THAT CAPTURED squid, as the huge manifestation of his obsession quickened his heart and fed blood back into his cold face, Sir Edward Burnett Tylor published his encompassing volume *Primitive Culture: Researches into the Development of Mythology, Philosophy, Religion, Language, Art, and Custom*, in which he officially declares, numerous times throughout the tome, Sun Worship and the Sun Gods of various cultures not objects of "religion," but objects of "myth."

Also in 1874, as Harvey doubtlessly exhaled onto his hands to warm them, the squid's stench burning his nostrils like some saline incense both perfect and terrible, Tepoztecatl, Aztec Pulque God and inspirer of ice cream, long since popularly obsolete since the sixteenth-century Spanish conquest of Mexico, yet still worshipped in various indigenous circles, was said to have failed the people, when, even after preappeased, he allowed the now-famed Locust Plague of 1874 to destroy much of their crops. The next year, though the devout were still asking the forgiveness of one they believed to be an angry god, a few less people—those who died of starvation for example—worshipped Tepoztecatl.

Also in 1874, the Newfoundland Inuit and Innu leashed some of their myths to those of the Anglo colonists, in an effort to "move forward." Old black cats could divine the future, and should be followed. The direction of the wind could most accurately be determined by decapitating a gray fox, tying the head with string, and dangling it from the branch of a chokecherry. If, while pregnant, a woman saw a hare, she would birth a harelipped child. As the cosmos resulted not from creation, but was a crumb of destruction, killing was an act of reverence. (A celestial muskrat filled her mouth with the cosmos in the wake of a universal flood and began choking on it. A wolverine saw this and blew air up her ass, and the muskrat spat up our world.) Dwarves and sprinting worms and mermen and witches who collected the entrails of men who laughed too much, and kayaking giants and their half-human half-dogs who live in their boot soles, and superwolves, and the nightmarish *anghiak*—ghostly abortions returned for revenge—merged with conversations about confederacy infrastructure. Scapulimancy, a doctrine of societal rule determined by the reading of old shoulder-blade bones, was on its last legs.

As Harvey, right there on the shore in 1874, even before conversing with the fishermen who captured the Devil-fish, began hatching a plan to transport the behemoth, much to the forthcoming dismay of his wife, Sarah, to his home, and then bathroom, the Europe that Harvey fled began to deal with a painful economic depression in what came to be known as its Year of Crisis. During this Year of Crisis, writer-philosopher Friedrich Nietzsche declared his support for authoritarian power in the form of Otto von Bismarck, and published the second and third volumes of his *Untimely Meditations*, in which he attacks man's dependence on history, including religious history, as a primary pathway to knowledge, believing that most of his fellows used religion as a way to avoid making decisions, and thereby taking the necessary attendant action.

In this way, Nietzsche, as Moses Harvey sneezed for the third time on that Newfoundland beach, sowed the seeds for his famous declaration, published eight years later in *The Gay Science*, that "Gott ist tot": *God is dead.*

ᘓ

CAN WE EVER REALLY KILL A MYTH? EVEN though the giant squid has long been proved actual, the beast retains the mythological narrative, can't shake its sea-monster designation. The legend lives on. Oddly enough, the giant squid, both mythologically, and actually, approaches immortality. From *Biological Perspectives on Human Pigmentation* by Ashley H. Robins (a text which postulates that "skin color is perhaps the most decisive and abused physical characteristic of humankind," but says nothing of that awful Chicago heatwave of 1995, during which variations in melanin determined which people lived where in the city, and, in turn, which people were more easily dispatched by the weather):

"Cephalopod melanin is invulnerable to decay and early in the 19th century, in the South of England, a 150-million-year-old squid was discovered whose own ink was used to make drawings of its remains (Fox & Vevers, 1960)."

The drawings, according to Harvey, were "shown to a celebrated artist [who] pronounced the sepia to be excellent, and inquired by what colourman it had been prepared . . . [not knowing that it] had been entombed in solid rock for countless ages."

Later, in 2009, another such discovery was made by British paleontologists who "cracked open what appeared to be an ordinary looking rock only to find the one-inch long black ink sac inside." The leader of this excavation, Dr. Phil Wilby, states, "We think that these creatures were swimming around during the Jurassic period and were turned to stone soon after death. It's called the Medusa effect . . . We felt that drawing the animal with [its still intact ink sac–which when dried is called *sepia*] would be the ultimate self-portrait."

ᔓ

BOTH HISTORY-OBSESSED MARINE BIOLOGISTS and marine-biology–obsessed historians now entertain the possibility that Moses Harvey invented the character of Little Tommy Picco for the sake of narrative, and the narrative's subsequent "immortality." Why was he compelled to do this? It was characteristic of Harvey to recycle material under different titles, but an outright fabrication? Was this typical as well? (His original account of the story, as told to the *New York Herald*, included no mention of Little Tommy Picco–the tentacle, according to his original account, was hacked off by one of the "men").

It seems that the exhilaration that Harvey felt upon attaining said tentacle was transferable to an audience only via the vehicle of a fabricated twelve-year-old boy. Certainly, this literary device lends Harvey's story a greater urgency and anxiety; a greater sense of nostalgia, and the nostalgic brew of dumb youthful courage and nonchalance. Is this what Harvey felt when two adult fishermen brought him that tentacle in 1873? Did Harvey, if only in his chest, become young again? Or did he merely long to be young again, and specifically *of* a place, *of* an ocean, as confident, and as confidently *at home,* as a boy named Picco? It seems this was Harvey's attempt to create what literary types dub *emotional truth.* Did Harvey have to fudge the facts in order to best transfer the truth of how he felt when that tentacle came upon him? Or: did he witness, in that tentacle, the burgeoning death of one myth and, in order to maintain the equilibrium of some larger truth–one dependent on amounts–felt driven to invent another?

೧

FROM THE *HALIFAX HERALD*, CHRISTMAS EVE, 1884:

"Were it not that [Harvey's] story . . . is told with such

statistical minuteness, one might readily imagine himself in a realm of romance."

ᔕ

IN THE *ST. JOHN'S DAILY NEWS*, NOVEMBER 1894, Major General Dashwood, who Moses Harvey defines as "a hopeless monomaniac on the subject of Newfoundland," publicly accuses Harvey of passing off fiction as nonfiction, calling him "a falsifier, and unworthy of being believed . . . [Everything he has published is] a scandalous falsehood."

ᔕ

IS THE ACT OF PERPETUATING "A SCANDALOUS falsehood," an act birthed in loneliness, in a sort of pain? Do we spin our tales, in part, to have some decent company, even though we're still alone in the room? Should we have no one with whom to commune, does our nature dictate that we create them, make them "real?" Without profound pain, can there be a God (or god), or a God (or god) Complex?

ᔕ

OF COURSE, EVEN HARVEY SOMETIMES HAD TO interrogate the narratives of his sources: "One man gave me a thrilling account of a narrow escape he and two others had on the coast of Labrador. The little vessel of some 25 or 30 tons . . . suddenly began to sink, until the deck was nearly on a level with the water. But there was no water in her hold to account for this."

ᔕ

STORY BEGETS STORY.

ᔕ

WHEN DASHWOOD ASKED HARVEY WHAT THEN, if he was real, became of Tommy Picco, Harvey was ready. "He became," Harvey answered nonchalantly, "a handsome strapping young fisherman and fearless seal hunter."

ᔕ

THE SAME *NEW YORK HERALD* ARTICLE THAT CITES Harvey's original account of the "Picco" escapade, also interrogates the "truth" as perpetuated by other sources:

> I opened two volumes of the new Encyclopedia Britannica and looked for the articles "Cuttle Fish" and "Devil Fish." In neither of these essays is there a single allusion to the gigantic cephalopod now under review. This great encyclopedia is only in the currency of its publication; for in a work of admitted general ability, pretending, too, to aim

as a specialty at great scientific precision and comprehensiveness, it would be difficult and unfair to assume that these papers are mere reprints from previous editions of the "Encyclopedia" that had never been retouched or subjected to revision. Under the heading of "Devil fish" the anonymous writer treats merely of the history and habits of that vulgar gourmand, the frog fish.

ᘓ

Fact as the product of editorial laziness.
Fact as subject to schedule, calendar.
Fact as taking great pleasure in consumption.
Fact as vulgar.
Fact as a changing, perhaps with a shrug, of the mind.

ᘓ

PAIN BEGETS CREATION, BEGETS POWER, BEGETS other pain.

ᘓ

ST. JOHN'S ITSELF IS FAMOUS FOR FABRICATIONS repeated to the point that they become truth. Local advertisements about the city's Water Street ran year after year declaring it "the oldest commercial street in the Americas," a blatantly untrue statement that is now, according to most Newfoundlanders, fact—another indelible, if capitalistic, pathway to immortality.

ᔓ

"AS THERE ARE NO RECORDS, WE CAN ONLY imagine," Joan Ritcey of the Centre for Newfoundland Studies says, "that the specimen was transported to St. John's harbor by boat. That would be the easiest way."

Moses Harvey, that 1874 morning, had walked all the way to Logy Bay, three miles from St. John's. He was not in the habit of walking that far, and did not realize that he had covered such a distance. Perhaps the distance would have occurred to him, if only in his body, as a small indefinable pain, had that giant squid not appeared like some horrible downed stormcloud, surrounded by bearded, red-cheeked men in orange slickers. Maybe he remembered that in Newfoundland English, *logy* means *heavy,* and that Logy Bay was so named since disproportionately large fish swam there.

I picture Harvey that morning, still exhausted after his giant-squid dream, unable to get out of his head the thought of those tentacles, arriving by horseback at his home just a handful of weeks ago, unable to shake the rumor, which he was unable during his lifetime to confirm, that some of the smaller tentacle was later cut up and fed to the fishermen's dogs, letting the front door swing shut, the squeak of it sounding to Sarah, who stood in the shadows watching her husband step out into the gray light, like a rat screaming, and he stepped down, over stone and matted weeds, wet with the early hour, onto the rubble that lined the shoulder of the street. In his chest, some quickening that needed calm. Some blurry ache in need of salve. The garage where those two men in fishing jackets drank from paper bags did not yet exist. The fathers and mothers of those two men in fishing jackets who drank from paper bags did not yet exist. No one alive then could have imagined that the Harvey home would later be painted hospital lavender.

Harvey headed, on some magnetic instinct, around the block toward Water Street, one of his favorites. A curious man, he would have known that he was walking down the oldest street in North America, but would not have interrogated the veracity of this designation. His hair and beard were snow-white. They caught the sun as it came through in shards. He walked almost formally erect.

The Water Street immigrants would have been setting up their tables, advertising their wares and services. Harvey would have overhead shouts and murmurs in English, French, Spanish, Portuguese, and Basque. He understood little of what he heard. He saw and smelled horses, and saw and smelled people, and saw and smelled a melting pot of breakfasts on plates and breakfasts in pots and breakfasts in mouths, steam escaping over the lips of children and old women and young men. He smelled the sea, and the dead fish for sale, which took on the smell that morning of the sea spoiling. If it were winter, after a snowfall, Harvey would not have been able to see the tops of the buried houses. He would not have been able to navigate the sidewalks, as there was no committee to clean them. He would have seen candles melting ovals into the frost on the shopfront windows. But it was not yet winter, and there was no ice to transluce the stubbled face of the tailor, noosed in yellow measuring tape, to whom he nodded as he passed.

Cracking his neck, he walked the 64 meters, the 188 steps it took to get to the corner of Temperance Street, passing, on the way, the rank fish stages that would later become Lansing Properties, Inc.: Furnished Condos Available Short/Long Term, and later become the Red Ochre Gallery, specializing in still lifes of flowers and furniture, and forearm-sized clay whale sculptures, and later become a lot-sized billboard for 99.1 FM: Newfoundland's #1 Hit Music Station, which runs such prize-bearing contests for listeners as What's in Bieber's Book Bag?: Guess the Items in the Bag and Win a Trip for Two to NYC!, and later become Hempware: Ecologically-Friendly Products, and later become Flower Child: Eco-Funky Kid Stuff.

He passed a policeman in a tall beaver hat, an officer who was infamous in St. John's for staking out the hillsides, tailing children with reckless reputations, and confiscating their sleds. Harvey heard a rumor that there was a storage room in the cellar of the Old Court House piled floor-to-ceiling with these sleds. He passed the trail that led to O'Dwyer's Cove, a popular local spot to go drowning, where folks lined up for hours with their buckets to draw water—dead-body water—from the old pump. In spite of this, diphtheria, appendicitis, diabetes, and tuberculosis remained rare in the local schoolrooms.

Before turning left, Harvey would have passed the chinaware shop run by Hannah Martin, cofounder of Devon Row, which later became the Seaman's Institute, which later became King George V Institute; and he would have passed the site that was to become S. O. Steele & Sons, Ltd., also owned by a descendant of the Martins, and he would have passed the site that was to become Martin Hardware, which later merged with Royal Stores Hardware to become, appropriately, Martin–Royal Stores Hardware.

And before turning left, Harvey would have passed the place that's now Britannia Teas and Gifts, where he could have purchased rooibos tea from my wife's home country, and BeeHouse teapots, Mrs. Bridges preserves, and souvenir tea cozies with googly-eyed squid sewn baby-blue into their middles, and then the provincial court where folks inside were being declared alternately guilty and innocent, and then the place that would become Blue on Water, Newfoundland's premier boutique hotel, which offers its guests squid-watching tours and is the darling of *Great Big Sea* magazine, and then the stretch of outposts that would later, on a hot day (87 degrees in the shade, high winds) in 1892 be engulfed in flames during St. John's Great Fire, which Harvey would also personally witness during another afternoon walk that submitted to some magnetic instinct, and about which he would say famously, "It was a bad day for a fire . . . Every circumstance combined to favor the progress of the destroyer."

And: "The torrent approached; the house next to [Devon] Row blazed up, and the blood-red tongues of fire shot out, licking the gable-end and mounting towards the roof."

And: "We held our breath, waiting for the final catastrophe; but the fiery bombardment did not take effect; the sparks flew off without getting a lodgement."

And: "Where yesterday stood the homes of 15,000 people, there were only ashes and debris, or walls and chimney stalks, ghastly in their nakedness. The wrecks of the fanes of religion stood out, [their] broken walls pointing heavenward, as if in mournful protest against the desecration that had been wrought."

And: "And the poor inhabitants, where were they? It made the heart ache to see the groups of men, women and children, with weary, blood-shot eyes and smoke-begrimed faces, standing over their scraps of furniture and clothing–some of them asleep on the ground from utter exhaustion–all with despondence depicted on their faces. They filled the parks and grounds around the city."

Though the city had been set ablaze thrice–by the French, by the Dutch, by its own Royal Navy–it was this 1892 blaze, and Harvey's penchant for appropriate adjectives, that inspired "greatness."

Harvey, still reaching himself for greatness, immortality, would have bypassed what is now called Harvey Road, then an unnamed, infrequently traveled spur off of Longs Hill, bypassing a row of small girls, sisters perhaps, milking a row of small cows, a bowlegged farmer leaning, perhaps, on his pitchfork, crumbs of hay dampening unnoticed under his tongue, passing the plot of land on which Ches's Famous Fish & Chips now stands, advertising All U Can Eat Calamari Baskets, and advertising Fried Cod Tongue Dinners: Your Choice of Chips or Rice, and Family Buckets with names like Trawl Tub and Captain's Mess, and the Bait Jack, and Boson's Scoff, and combo meals for the indecisive ("Can't decide between chicken and fish?") called Fin & Feather. He would have bypassed the plot of land on which–my favorite–Bacalao:

Nouvelle Newfoundland Cuisine now stands, advertising its "hyperlocal food," and he would have passed what was to become the Cotton Club where, "Our Girls Party Naked," and the Sundance Saloon and the red stone mercantile building that would later become the YellowBelly Brewery and the Anglican Church that later served as a refuge during the 1892 fire before it too was engulfed in flames, its Gothic architecture seething to ash, its roof crashing inward, rebuilt years afterward, and years after that, would open a Tea Room in the Crypt and would paint the crypt walls Tuscan yellow and furnish it with sky-blue plastic chairs and tables with pink cloths.

On Temperance (named for the movement forged by the Newfoundland Irish working class), Harvey would have walked the 91 meters back to Duckworth, where he would have seen the last of the early street cows (as it was against the law to drive them through the city after 8:00 A.M.), and a family of five hacking up a harp seal after the morning hunt, and he may have retrieved one of its fallen whiskers and picked a crumb of last night's dinner from his molar with it, and the residential lot on which Samuel Garrett, just a few years later, would build the famed, conjoined Garrett houses as wedding gifts to his four daughters, number 31 of which would many years later house Oceans Ltd. Research Company whose mission is to "improve safety at sea," and provide "marine weather forecasting services," and maintain the "monitoring of fish health," and plots of seagrassland that were to become condos and parking lots and Powers Surplus and Salvage.

The ocean crashed into the Narrows. Harvey likely shivered as he turned left on Duckworth as a wind tunnel bridging St. John's and sea opened up, and he pulled his neck deeper into his coat and he passed the wind tunnel and pushed his neck out into the air again. He ran his fingertips along the brick of the Tobacco Company. He collected the dust of it beneath his fingernails, and picked it out with other fingernails.

He passed, in his words, "The beautiful shops full of valuable goods; the stores behind containing thousands of barrels of flour and provisions of all kinds; the fish stores; the wharves, which it had cost immense sums to erect..." He passed the pile of rubble that the Total Abstinence Society was busy cobbling into their three-story headquarters in which they would later denounce the consumption of alcohol, especially by those Newfoundlanders who worked in the fishing industry, men who would become objects of discrimination to those Abstinence Society members of the upper classes, who, in discussing the habits of the local fishermen, claimed, "a trial of strength had been made between the 'workies'... who subsisted exclusively on tea, coffee, and cold water at their meals, and those who took spirits in the usual way; and the men of more temperate liquids could do a third more work (and actually did it)..."

And Harvey kicked at this rubble, and he passed the future site of the Nickel Theatre, erected by the Benevolent Irish Society in 1907 and which usurped the Lumiere's Cinematographe at the Methodist College Hall, where Harvey, in December of 1897, less than four years before his death, saw his first moving picture. He passed the Star of the Sea Hall, whose mission it was to provide "spiritual advantages [to its fishermen] members," and he passed the clerk, the draper, the lawyer, the sailmaker, the block-maker, this season's club dance hall, a vacant red house rented by a dozen young men where every night from eight until twelve for sixpence apiece, boys and girls would whirl and dip and kiss and make plans, their entry fee split among the proprietors, the constable doorman, and the fiddler.

He walked past the sail-loft used nightly for theatrical performances, bazaars, raffles, and card parties, beyond what would become the Duckworth B&B but was now a swell of earth upon which couples laid their blankets for morning picnics of fried fish and tea, the younger of which stretched their bodies toward kisses, and Harvey wiped his nose, stared at the long rows of red stone chimneys, and the blackbirds that threaded them with the gulls, scavenging each other's morning catches, and passed the watchmaker's shop that would become Asian Taste, and the tented Basque market that would become Courtyard by Marriott, and the toymaker's shop that would become the Duke of Duckworth pub, which has seen the patronage of the likes of David Bowie and Huey Lewis sans News.

Harvey turned right on Cavendish Square, stepping over scraps of furniture and clothing, and remembered his age–fifty-four–and likely realized that he was going to skip lunch today, which he did not like to do, and he walked northwest through the square in which merchant after merchant peddled things made of wood and steel and iron and fish, grounds that later would give in to hotel row–the Fairmount, the Rosewood, the Sheraton–the latter of which is always booked due to niche gatherings like the Conference on the Dynamics of the Earth's Radiation Belts and Inner Magnetosphere, and the RBC Bank, and the Rotary Club, and Hair Factory, and the Wig Shop, and LeMoine's.

Taking a right on Kings Bridge Road, passing the small residences–their mansard roofs and bonnet-topped dormers, the occasional discarded flipper, discarded pieces of mail, O'Brien's stable with its sweet stink of horse urine, the shaggy animals inside shivering flies from their flanks, the drapery business, Terra Nova Bakery, the

Avalon Iron Foundry, a carriage hauling a cart of golden codfish chased by a pack of dogs, smiling children, weeping children, a black seal coughing, a candy-shop sign in the shape of a polar bear, the merchant living above it leaning from his window to clean his pipe, the ash of it collecting between the polar bear's cherrywood paws, the Old Kinkora Place, its Queen Anne Revival architecture, its steep-hipped roof, pilasters and porch, he thought he saw, carved into its second-story window pediments, a series of sea horses he may have mistaken for kelpies, the objects of a Celtic folktale he remembered his father telling him; anyone who dared try to ride a kelpie, Harvey would have recalled, would forever be unable to get off its back, even as it shifted shape, even as it became, in some tellings, the embryonic kraken, growing to attack ships, to grudgingly lend its tentacles to science. Maybe Harvey sneezed, and maybe he was a little afraid and getting hungry, afraid of his appetite, his obsession, his addiction, his disease, afraid that now that he had touched the tentacles of a giant squid, he would never be able to disembark–he was on its back now, of that he would have been certain.

All he perhaps remembered seeing along the half-mile stretch of Kings Bridge Road to Kenna's Hill was his shoes, brown hide over stone, and he would not have remembered the land that would later be razed for Kings Bridge Service Station and Captain's Quarters Hotel, and the vacant railyard that would become the site of the Prince of Wales Rink for indoor skating, which, after burning down during WWII, was rebuilt as Memorial Stadium, host to the historic hockey game between the St. John's Caps and the Soviet Red Army, and an address by Pope John Paul II, and which boasts underground parking, and escalators, and Cartveyors, three things Moses Harvey never dreamt of.

He crossed the lawn of the old British military complex, the Commissariat, on which at least a dozen children have historically vomited after eating squid, and on which, as I decades later passed, a beautiful couple married, flanked by the property's giant greenhouse and green picket fence as Van Morrison's "Tupelo Honey" played, and Harvey trudged up Kenna's Hill, not thinking of Sarah at all, back at the house on Devon Row, wondering if he was coming home for lunch or not, up what would become a major artery, big-box store haven, strip mall central, home of the Carpet Factory Super-Store (WE'VE GOT MORE THAN JUST CARPET!), up along the cool bank of Quidi Vidi Lake, where he more than once kissed his wife, where the city's refugees would later flee to safety in 1892 after the Anglican Church burnt down, setting up a camp of tents, and Harvey huffed up and along Logy Bay Road, marveling at the seabirds in the sea meadow that would later become a sea of Ultramar gasoline banners, the seabirds themselves realizing perhaps, even in their bird brains, that their populations thicken over bodies of water that have higher concentrations of giant squid, as they exploit the beasts' edible and crumb-sized ejecta. And Harvey clambered past St. Mark's Church, its facade slat-battered, its interior not yet wheelchair-accessible, not yet bearing the sign on its door reading NO SCENTED PRODUCTS PLEASE! ST. MARK'S STRIVES TO BE A SCENT-FREE CHURCH, and he trekked past St. Thomas' Anglican Church, now painted a coastal blue-gray and white, and advertising HOLY COMMUNION EVERY WED. AT 10AM IN THE GARRISON ROOM, and boasting a sign declaring EVERYONE WELCOME, though when I tried to go inside, every single door was locked, and Harvey could smell the sea, the dwarf spruce and fir, the peat, the juniper, the tamarack, the berry shrubs, the salted fish air-drying, the icebergs, and he passed the hills which led to cliffs, and the short wooden fences, and he crossed Newfoundland Drive, where Breen's Superette would later open and sell warm desserts called Apple Flip, and brands of candy bars that neither I nor my wife nor Moses Harvey grew up with, and he quickened his pace without knowing why, and this may have frightened him too, his body running without his brain, carrying him like some displaced kelpie, like some spokesperson for the Irish Diaspora, like an obsession that doesn't quite take the pain away but bandages it, and he heaved air into his lungs and passed a skinny tree that would later be fat, and his knees may have begun to hurt as he walked on and up and felt the sea wind caress his right side, and the breeze off of Virginia Lake caress his left, and he passed the lot that would later house the unfortunately abbreviated MANAL (Muslim Association of Newfoundland and Labrador), and, though he smelled and felt it for a while now, he came upon a view of the sea upon which Seaview Auto Service would later base its name. And Moses Harvey heard, in the distant woods–the ash and pine and oak and aspen and poplar and willow–the commingled shuffle of reindeer and caribou, of wolf and black bear, of black fox and silver fox and gray fox and red fox, of beaver and marten, of weasel and mouse, of bat and rat, and musquash and hare, all waiting, aware, to be trapped by trappers and stripped of their skin, and Moses Harvey saw what should never be: grouse running with geese and auks flying with loons; he saw a puffin walking like a guillemot, and a gull quacking like a duck; and Moses Harvey turned off the road, cut through the dunes and beachgrass and lots and yards, the patches of red clover and white clover and vetch, away from the land beasts and the property we share with them, and his hands may have had to touch the ground to keep himself on his feet, and he may have stained his palms with the fruits of the plants, red with hurtleberry and whortleberry and partridgeberry and chokecherry, and the little white ant's egg of the fruit of the trailing maidenhair, supersaturated with saccharine; and he tumbled through lilies, through blue iris, through flowers with names like dog's tooth violets, cow cracca, Solomon's seal, Jacob's ladder, lady's saddle, wild lupine, bellflower, coltsfoot, heart's ease, columbine; he saw caterpillars hung like soft tamarind in the trees, denuding the leaves to their veins; and he saw boys and girls dragging rowboats, and boys and girls playing concertinas and cornets and flutes, and he saw elderly folks watching them play, slouched onto the gump-heads of piers and on piles of lumber, and he could have sworn he saw ducks in the air speaking in tongues to ducks on the earth, and then he was on rocks, stumbling downhill over them and then he was on smaller stones, and he may have missed his mother and he may have missed his father, and he felt that cold pins-and-needles rain, that rain with gumption, and his heart began to speed, and he felt frightened, and he was at the shore, finally at the shore, and he smelled it, before he knew what it was he was smelling, and his nose begun, as it did from time to time, to bleed, and he may have put his hand to his mouth to catch the blood, and he may have let it fall to the beach to mix with the rain and the sea, and he may not have missed his mother, and he may not have missed his father, and his world may have gone orange, and he would have seen the squid and he would have seen the squid and he would have seen the squid . . .

൴

OF COURSE HIS HEART WAS RACING, AND IF HE had been clutching pompons instead of his own cracked hands, he would have cheered aloud and wiggled those decorative balls of fluff and attempted the splits, but Harvey later wrote, "I remember to this day how I stood on the shore of Logy Bay, gazing on the dead giant . . . I resolved that only the interests of science should be considered."

൴

I SAW NO SQUID AT LOGY BAY, BUT I FELT HARvey, and those fishermen in the sea-flattened gray beach stones, the craggy ochre cliffs spattered with white gulls and puffins and their nests and their feces and their screaming. The crew-cut grass and rickety spruce. In skinny clouds that have never moved faster. In the cold ocean. In the 4.4 seconds between wave crashes. In the families gathering capelin into their red buckets and green buckets and blue buckets, to use as bait, as fetid garden fertilizer, as supper. In the scuba-diving boys. In the pregnant woman picking up shells for her toddler son.

In the toddler trying, and failing, to skip stones. In the black and white cat on a red leash. In the tour bus idling in the parking lot, the seniors on board slack-mouthed, unsure of whether they should be taking photos or naps. In the woman on the hillside, circled by gulls, holding to her chest the silver urn that she's not yet ready to empty.

൘

AS MOSES WOULD HAVE SEEN THE SQUID, SARAH Harvey would have fallen back to sleep, would have had the dream again—the one that I feel compelled to impose upon her—of her husband walking, entranced, unblinking, beyond her. This time, in the dream, their Devon Row house had a rolling green yard, something of the Irish countryside, and upon it, Sarah, implacably lonely, hosted a lawn party for the blank-faced locals. Through these locals, each holding a plate heaped with hors d'oeuvres, Moses walked, Red Rover–style, toward the sea with what appeared to be a crumb of raspberry mustard at the corner of his mouth. A woman in a blue pheasant hat and blue pheasant voice fluttered, "Raspberry mustard? But when did *that* become available?"

Overhead, twelve gulls flapped their wings, and this woman flapped her chin, and she sighed, and the four ladies surrounding her sighed in unison.

Maybe Sarah woke then, and wiped her eyes, and

wondered where her children were, and didn't have to wonder where Moses was, and before the dream steamed away, she thought the raspberry mustard wasn't raspberry mustard, but a speck of giant squid. Sniffing at the air for anything Irish, she rolled from the bed and, with both hands, began smoothing the sheets. The silver tea service—a gift from the church—sat as yet unused on the armoire. It reflected something Sarah would not have recognized as her own body.

൴

TODAY, NO BEES, NO BIRDS. NO ONE ANSWERED the door to the Harvey home that night I drunkenly rung the bell, so, this morning, a few days later, I set the alarm for 6:00 A.M. and try before breakfast (I'd scoped out a nice spot just up the street from Devon Row—the Classic Cafe East—where I was eagerly anticipating downing a huge meal of fish and brewis as salve for what I guessed would be another failed attempt at finding the wizard behind the bad purple curtain). The foghorns. The fog. The peeling paint. The morning condensation. People happy, and people in pain. Running, limping. People who can manage their feelings silently, and people who are compelled to whistle and wail. The garage across the street still closed, the men likely sleeping, dreaming alcoholic dreams, dreaming perhaps, of twine shops and mummers and squid and carrots. An inordinate number of women wearing hospital scrubs parade past.

I climb the three steps and am beginning to feel at home on this threshold. It's so predictable, the ensuing failure. And comfortable. I ring the bell. I shrug at no one. I wait. Just as I'm about to step down into the street, toward my breakfast of salt cod with onion, scrunchion (crispy pork fat), and dampened mashed-up biscuit that will remind me of the *matzo brei* recipe that passed through Dorothy to my mother from some unknown generational origin on the bottom of another kind of sea–yes: just as I'm about to step down into the street toward this kind of breakfast, I hear a lock uncouple itself from its harbor, watch swim behind the frosty windowglass the sort of movement that can only be described as a surfacing.

ᘓ

MOSES AND SARAH HARVEY WERE HOMESICK for Ireland. As Carolyn Lambert, of Memorial University of Newfoundland, writes: "Between 1840 and 1886, the Catholic community in St. John's evolved from a largely immigrant one defined by an Irish ethnic identity and world view, to one where Catholicism and not ethnicity became the basis of community solidarity. Members identified primarily as Newfoundland-born Catholics, and it was their religion that provided them with an essential link to their Irish past. Although a romantic attachment to Ireland remained, they were far from the homes of their fathers."

Further, Harvey and Sarah were Presbyterian, adhering to "the Calvinist theological tradition within Protestantism," making them a minority even within the Newfoundland-based Irish Diaspora, as, Lambert continues, "demographically, St. John's was also distinctive because Catholics were counterbalanced by a Protestant population that was of English rather than Irish descent. This makes the context of study different from other urban areas of British North America, where Catholics formed a minority and Irish Protestants formed a large portion of the population." And so, in St. John's, the Harveys shared a religious commonality not with their own countryfolk, but with a minority population of English, who, back "home," made subhumans and slaves of the Harveys' grandparents. (The Newfoundland Irish students even had to send their exams back to England to be graded). So Harvey developed a practical (but perhaps misguided) rather than passionate take on religion. "Denominational zeal," he said, "perhaps furnishes a stimulus to educational effort."

Surely, Moses Harvey said this with a sigh of resignation. Moses Harvey often felt, as does my wife, now feeling never entirely at home in either South Africa or

America, homeless. My wife often tells me that home has nothing to do with how long one resides in a particular place. She tells me: a persistent sense of homelessness is a kind of pain—one that houses a cadre of fears. Surely, such a condition could be expressed only in a private manner, in a style of mythmaking that may appear, to the rest of us, as fetish. The search for *home*, like our expressions of pain, becomes even more private, and inexpressible to many, myself included.

~

AND SO, WHICH IS GREATER: THE PAIN OF THE monster (the pain of the myth) or the pain of those who require their monsters? Are these mythologies, in part, the stories of our collective, or collected, pain? Or our communal hope—the kind that feeds sweat and sleeplessness? Or, to qualify, is mythology the expression of our greatest semi-imagined fears, our dumbest pain in the face of that big hope unrealized? Or is this all just a dream about raspberry mustard?

~

HARVEY KNEW: WHEN WE MYTHOLOGIZE THE Other, we subjugate it and claim ownership. Even if we label the object of our mythmaking as superior to us (as in the case of the Sun God, the Pulque God, the

Judeo-Christian God), we still foster an inequality, the sort of which allows us the power when we deem necessary—whether culturally or individually, whether physically or rhetorically—to kill it. Later, after disseminating the photograph of his fateful squid, Harvey mused, apparently second-guessing his drive to bring the beast to the world, "Am I a dog that I should do this thing?"

~

SAYS TEPOZTECATL, LOOSELY TRANSLATED FROM the Nahuatl, *Here, in this wind, even the Rapture is a kind of pain.*

Part Four

WE'RE COMING TO A HEAD WIND

GOUGH ISLAND, IN THE SOUTH ATLANTIC, IS volcanic, and Darren Gough was a fabulous ballroom dancer, and John Gough was a blind experimental philosopher whose father dyed wool, and who conducted studies on the heat released by stretched rubber bands, as detected by the lips to which he pressed band after band . . . , and John Bartholomew Gough was a reformed bookbinder, cheap-theater ballad singer, and drunk, who became a famous lecturer on temperance reform, and Richard Gough was an antiquarian who created the Gough Map, the oldest surviving route map of Great Britain, and Stephen Gough walked the length of Great Britain naked, and spent six years in prison for it, and the Gough bunting faces extinction as the house mouse population eats all of its food, and Gough means *red* in Welsh, and Gough

Plastics makes tanks (including the MegaTrough™) to hold water or molasses or chemicals, and Arthur Gough answers the door to Moses Harvey's home and says to me—or *at* me—before he says anything else, "Because they couldn't feed their dogs, they ate them."

It's early in the morning—before coffee. I think I'm seeing ghosts, and I can't imagine what Arthur Gough thinks he's seeing, as he shakes the cobwebs from his head, blinks fiercely as if coming up from some dark watery place to the cruelty of the sun, and his fingers are pencil long and just as skinny and shaking, and his glasses frames are huge and as purple as the bad Devon Row paint job. His fontanel is as vulnerable as the bunting that bears his surname, infantile with a few white hairs riding sidesaddle in the wind. The thin magenta lining of his olive-green and beige plaid sportcoat has come loose and is hanging frayed from his shirtsleeves—*like* extra shirtsleeves—over his wrists. Beneath, a rank yellow silk shirt hangs misbuttoned, the collar of which bears orange amoebas like a white popcorn ceiling infected with old water stains. A blue pen flops about in his breast pocket. His too-big-in-the-waist greenish cuffed slacks are cinched with a scuffed brown belt, and his slippers are red and blue plaid, a feeble platform, this man surely about to topple back into ghosthood, or ocean-floor, or down the three steps into my arms. He must be ninety. He's drooling. My own mouth opens like the mail slot. He shakes his head, clearing it, realizing, perhaps, where he is. I'm trying to do the same. The foghorn. Before his head stops shaking, and before I can say a word, he says, his voice small and feminine, "I know who you are. I got your note."

I reach my hand forward. I say hello. The garage across the street remains closed, hatching its secrets in malign paper-baggery.

"I'm not much of a history buff," Arthur Gough says, "so I'm not much interested."

Behind me, and in front of Arthur Gough, a Pomeranian, attached via red leash to a barrel-chested man in a striped shirt, black beret, and skull-and-crossbones forearm tattoos, shits a peanut-in-the-shell on the sidewalk, its stench asserting itself briefly as vinegary disappointment, before the owner, with a peach Puffs Plus, cleans it from the concrete.

Gough wipes his lips with the back of his hand, but still, they seem wet. He holds onto the threshold for support. I'm about to say something about having come a very long way, about man as a born explorer, but I don't think Gough would sympathize. I'm still thinking about starving people eating starving dogs, and then having no transportation out of some godforsaken barrens. I'm still thinking about the things with which myth converges, and what happens to both as a result. I'm still hearing foghorns, and burping up last night's caribou, when Arthur Gough tells me that he'll tell me the little that he knows.

ᔕ

ONE OF THE PARTS CONTRIBUTING TO THE ENTIRE chaotic mechanism responsible for bringing that squid to the Harvey bathroom was the fishing hoist. Though Joan Ritcey (of Memorial University's Centre for Newfoundland Studies) could find for me no documents pertaining to period fishing hoists, and though the nature and manufacturer of the hoist Harvey (and his crew of various unknowns) used to lift the giant squid from beach to boat in Logy Bay, and then from boat to horse-drawn flatbed back in St. John's, remains a mystery, we can speculate.

We know this: ancient Egyptians used counterweighted levers to lug massive amounts of water to irrigation ditches upon which their agricultural success depended. Devising a ramp composed of sandbags, the ancient Greeks hoisted the 2,000 columns to the top of the Temple of Artemis at Ephesus. Devising what became known as the Archimedean screw, Archimedes was able to lift great buckets of water and other things heavy. The monks of the Abbey of Mont-St-Michel, in thirteenth-century coastal France, invented a treadmill-based hoist, which was powered not by manual labor (as was the Archimedean screw), but by donkeys. This is, perhaps, the earliest example of the

transfer of labor, and thereby the transfer of power, from human animal to nonhuman animal.

King Louis XV, in 1743, demanded of his underlings the construction of a personal hoist between his palace bedroom and his mistress's small flat. In London, in 1823, fifty years before Harvey secured those squid arms, customers would pay to stand on an ascending platform to view the city from a height. Ten years later, in the Harz Mountains, miners were lowered into and then raised from the mine via a series of reciprocating rods that reached 250 feet into the shaft. These examples were the prototypes for contemporary elevators and escalators, hoists to haul ourselves. In this way, we first became loads, became the cargo.

In 1835, Frost and Strutt built, in England, the earliest steam lift, driven by counterweights and belts. Ten years later, Sir William Thompson devised the first hydraulic crane. The crane was employed by dockworkers in Newcastle in order to load and unload cargo, much of which included fish.

We can guess that a similar device, employing a chain-and-pulley system, employing hoisting tackles and gear tubs and stern-whips and bow-whips, was the device that allowed Harvey and crew to raise the giant squid from the shores of Logy Bay, where, before it was dropped onto the deck of the boat chosen to transport it, it hung there in midair like a shower curtain, like ten skinny people on an escalator, ascending, as if, to some mythological Better Place.

☙

HOW WE WILLFULLY DELUDE OURSELVES INTO an inability to empathize: into believing that we're not cargo; into calling it an *elevator*, even when we're going down.

☙

JOHN CROSBIE, NEWFOUNDLAND POLITICIAN, who *almost*, according to the locals, became prime minister of Canada, said, "There's a great myth in Newfoundland about the fisherman. He's a folk hero and can do no wrong. In fact, he's just as much a scoundrel as fishermen anywhere."

~

IT'S HARD NOT TO IMAGINE THE FISHERMEN, IN 1874, unfolding from their bunks on this boat at 2 A.M., preparing their gear at some coral first light, beginning their twenty-hour workday. These fishermen made $1,400 in a good year, $300 in a bad one. These fishermen cursed and spat coffee spit as they navigated the boat traffic, the boats that years later nostalgic types would describe as "romantic"–the dories and barques and brigantines, and square-riggers and fore-and-afters. They would breathe in the steam of the steamboats and launch their hot saliva at vessels with names like *Spitfire*, howl at the *Wolf*, dare the *Bloodhound* to track them. They would stare down and scoff at such steamboats that romantic newspapermen described as "what seemed to be a ship on fire, with a great curling black cloud of smoke vomiting forth from the depths of her hold" like squid parts from a sperm whale, and what holy newspapermen described as "like the bush which Moses saw on the plains of Horeb," and what other newspapermen described as "this strange monster of the deep, advanc[ing] steadily, no sails . . . set to catch the wind."

These fishermen somehow stayed on their feet, as the boat, its sides and ends flaring, smacked down even the most murderous of the waves. They somehow remained standing on the sanded timbers sawn from the thickest roots of native tree fields, pushing from the earth like compound fractures. Though it was tradition after the day's catch, no one played the accordion. On the off-season, the fishermen stored their boats six deep. From a distance, the mechanisms that carried them looked almost delicate, like tea saucers.

These fishermen are exhausted. Their boats will go extinct. Their boats will be the subject of academic honors theses, Canadian folklore classes, complicated essays with simple titles called "What Makes a Good Boat?" According to the essay's interview of a veteran boat-builder, "Well, what makes a good boat is a good head, because most of the time we're coming home, we're coming to head wind."

~

"IT'S PRIVATE," HE SAYS, "IT'S A PRIVATE HOME." Gough seems pissed off that I even suggested it. Still, I go on begging.

"Mr. Gough. Sir. Please. I've come such a long way to research this. A fourteen-hour ferry through the North Atlantic. Fog you wouldn't believe. Please. If only you'd allow me to come in and see the bathroom. The one where the squid hung."

Arthur Gough never knew about the squid that once

hung in his shitter. Never knew of Harvey's obsession. His family moved in "in . . . let's see . . . it must've been 1946 now–1946."

Gough moved in at nineteen, or younger, or older . . . let's see . . . with his parents, his two sisters, his brother, all long dead now. He was appointed to a bank job, or a job fishing in Trinity Bay, or he joined the Newfoundland Commission of Civil Service. Gough never married, never had children.

"That's about all I can tell you," he says. He seems a little afraid of me.

"I'd only take two minutes, tops, if I could just take a quick look . . ."

Gough stretches himself out to fill the doorway. This is pathetic, meager. I could sneeze this man to the ground. Still, the doorway is full of him. I imagine him at 6 or 19, baiting a lure, locking a vault, paving a road.

"Yes. We got your note. It's private. It's a private home. I'd rather not show you in. I'm not a historically minded person, you see . . ."

"Please? Just the bathroom. Sir."

"There are four bathrooms."

"May I . . ."

"*Four* bathrooms. Six bedrooms, and four bathrooms."

I close my mouth.

"We know why you're here. We got your note."

I open my mouth. How can this old man living alone keep a four-bathroom, six-bedroom home clean?

"Do you live alone, sir?"

Gough stiffens. "Yes. My family's all dead. Long dead . . ."

"But you said 'We,' sir. *We* got your note . . . ?"

"Yes."

"Who are the *we*, sir? Is there someone else in the house?"

Gough touches his scalp. His fingers leave divots.

"It's me and my brother. It's just my brother."

"But your brother's dead, sir?"

"He's dead, yes. Oh, long dead, now."

Everything Faulknerian seems to ride in with the fog, seems somehow right in place here, way up north. Sweat and bones rattle with the foghorns. The long-dead still have their own bedrooms here.

"But . . ."

Gough sighs, impatient, as if he's enduring my stupidity. I am panhandler and pest. He has to give me something if I'm to go away. He realizes this. His body slackens. He drops his arms from the doorframe.

"Fine," he says like a stubborn child. "In the backyard of this home were two long, walled galleries. My family replaced them with stained-glass enclosures. Moses Harvey was sitting on the railing of the gallery. There were two long galleries, you see? Long, walled galleries. My family replaced them. Now, these stained-glass enclosures. Moses Harvey fell off the back gallery. He was sitting on the railing one morning, and he tumbled off backwards. There were two. Two galleries. Moses Harvey threw himself off the railing of the gallery. Backwards. It wasn't a long fall, but it was enough. Moses Harvey killed himself by throwing himself off of the gallery. It was a suicide here. In the backyard. And now, we have stained glass . . ."

ᔓ

WE ALL FEEL A MEASURE OF THE DIASPORA. Most of us are out of our native waters. We keep close company with our family demons and ghosts that, to others, seem wistful and anecdotal. We can't escape them. I can't, just as Moses Harvey couldn't. At least we both found the giant squid.

ᔓ

FROM THE *ILLUSTRATED LONDON NEWS: THE WORLD of Science*, "Giant Squid: The Quest for the Kraken" by W. J. Rees, D.Sc., November 26, 1949: "[The giant squid] is the straggler, driven far from its normal haunts, which comes to grief on our shores."

~

LATE IN OUR CORRESPONDENCE–AWKWARDLY late–after I asked her a series of questions about the Centre for Newfoundland Studies' documents regarding the living descendants of Moses Harvey–who they are, whether they still live in the area or have moved on, whether they have reunions (like the ones Charles Darwin's descendants have), whether Harvey's children (or Sarah, for that matter) were affected in any way by Harvey's obsessions, and after such questions remained unanswered in her email replies, Joan Ritcey finally, reluctantly admits, "I have never read or heard of the family's interaction with Harvey. There are several great great grandchildren in town [St. John's]. I am one of them. We know each other but have never met for a reunion in his name."

I sent a series of follow-up emails, asking her about the other descendants; what it means to her to be a descendant, and what that means within the context of St. John's; and how, if at all, the giant squid, and Harvey's legacy, play their roles in the lives of her living family members, both implicitly and explicitly.

These, for her own good reasons, she chose not to answer.

~

JOAN RITCEY'S GRANDMOTHER (AND MOSES AND Sarah Harvey's granddaughter), Muriel Harvey Ritcey, was interviewed in the 1960s by Memorial University professor, marine biologist, and giant squid obsessive Dr. Frederick Aldrich. Aldrich asked questions about Moses Harvey. Presumably, his heart quickened as he asked them, and as he imagined the words he would later write: "Harvey had indeed brought these mammoth invertebrates from the realm of myth to the world of monstrous reality."

Aldrich died in 1991. Until that date, he held the title Moses Harvey Professor of Marine Biology. And the title of managing editor of the *Journal of Cephalopod Biology*. His papers are still with his widow Marguerite Aldrich, who has little interest, for her own good reasons, in releasing them.

ᘓ

WE DO KNOW THAT ALDRICH BELIEVED THAT every third decade the giant squid show up in great numbers along the coast of Newfoundland, a theory that many other marine biologists greeted with scorn and, while drinking after their hours in their labs, ridiculed: *every 30 years, when the moon is full in these here parts . . .*

Aldrich was also often scorned for his belief that giant squid are attracted to the color red, a color he would paint all of his squid jigs, a color that Newfoundland fishermen, unsure as to whether this was truth or superstition, refused to paint their boats.

൜

ALDRICH UNCOVERED A FASCINATING CONNECTION between the obsessions of clergymen and the giant squid. "Though not exclusively the domain of ecclesiastics," not only were Moses Harvey and Portugal Cove Reverend M. Gabriel and Olaus Magnus obsessed with the animal, but so was Norwegian Protestant Bishop Erik Ludvigsen Pontoppidan, who, two hundred years after Magnus's death, stole the late Swede's thunder and claimed that *he himself* "invented" the kraken, and claimed that it was the "size of a floating island" with horns "as long as a ship's mast." As Magnus was born in 1490, and Pierre Denys de Montfort, considered the first scientist to engage the giant squid, began his inquiries only in 1783, it can be said that the mythological giant squid belonged to the church for nearly three hundred years before science began to interrogate.

൜

ONE SPECIES OF GIANT SQUID WAS NAMED *ARCHIteuthis monachus*, or "sea monk."

൬

ALDRICH ADORED THE EPIC 1926 POEM "THE Cachalot" by Newfoundland's own E. J. "Ned" Pratt, which details a fight to the death between a kraken and a sperm whale, and is said to sit upon an odd subtext of both religious apocalypse and evolutionary themes, and has been described by critics as anything from "a romantic excursion into mythology" to "in the best sense, juvenile." The poem, dedicated to "the boys of the stag parties," kisses its own metrical bicep and coos, "Out on the ocean tracts, his mamma / Had, in a north Saghalien gale, / Launched him, a four-ton healthy male, / Between Hong Kong and Yokohama."

൬

ALDRICH ALSO LOVED AND OFTEN QUOTED Elizabeth Barrett Browning's poem "Lord Walter's Wife," which commences, "'But where do you go?' said the lady, while both sat under the yew, / And her eyes were alive in their depth, as the kraken beneath the sea-blue."

൬

APPEARING DOWNRIGHT ELLIOTT NESS-Y IN HIS fedora and overcoat and Dragnet tie, and tight jaw, Aldrich squatted over the corpse of a giant squid in a photo taken at White Bay in October 1964. He felt that advertising was important in getting the word out about the beast, mentioning of the corpse over which he squatted in that photo that "the specimen was towed ashore perhaps for no other reason than to prove that such an animal existed." With his ad campaign "offering $30 for the bodies of super squid," Aldrich secured five squid bodies throughout 1964 and 1965, confirming, he stressed, his "30 year cycle" hypothesis. Another ad campaign involved the distribution of WANTED! DEAD OR ALIVE! posters of the giant squid, urging "great care" and promising that "rewards are offered."

ᔕ

SOON AFTER THAT PHOTO WAS TAKEN, ALDRICH telephoned the Toronto-based "squid artist" Glen Loates (who had painted for a magazine the image of a giant squid battling a sperm whale) and complained over the phone that Loates didn't correctly capture the magnitude of the squid's eye. A feverish and excited three-hour conversation ensued, causing Aldrich to completely miss Evensong at the Anglican Cathedral of St. John the Baptist.

ᔕ

DURING THE CONVERSATION, ALDRICH WAS doubtlessly excited, scratching at his grizzled beard and wiping the mounting sweat from his huge forehead, as he settled back into his chair and lit cigarette after cigarette, eyeing his office's decorations—the porcelain busts of Sherlock Holmes and Dr. Watson (Aldrich self-identified as a Sherlockian), the oil painting of St. Thomas More, the electron micrograph of a chambered nautilus shell, the jars of formalin stuffed with flaccid, yellowed scraps of giant squid tentacles and beaks, the framed homily on the wall: *THE OCEAN'S BOTTOM IS MORE INTERESTING THAN THE MOON'S BEHIND.*

ᘓ

TOWARD THE END OF THE PHONE CALL, ALDRICH persuaded Loates to paint the WANTED! poster.

ᘓ

"I DO WHAT I DO TO THE BEST OF MY ABILITIES," Loates told Aldrich.

ᘓ

LOATES STARTED PAINTING AT AGE SIX, INSPIRED by the cemetery adjacent to his childhood home in which the burgeoning boy painter became fascinated not only with the shapes of gravestones and carved monuments, but also with the "living world" he discovered "amongst the grasses, and weeds, and trees" of the human dead. Ten years later, at age sixteen, Loates, after having finished Jules Verne's *Twenty Thousand Leagues Under the Sea*, sheathed in a sweat colder than a crypt, attempted to paint his first architeuthid.

ᘓ

"TO LOOK AT A SQUID'S EYES IS LIKE LOOKING into infinity," Loates said.

೧

LOATES CLAIMS HE WAS NOT DISAPPOINTED when, after accompanying Aldrich on a giant-squid expedition, they failed to witness the creature "in the depths of the ocean." Next time, Loates said, eyes on his loafers, richly bearded, they'd have to bring more bait (the giant cages filled with tuna were not enough), go down a whole lot deeper, and bring along an extra vessel. Eyes still down, Loates continued, his voice beginning to waver, almost, it seems, becoming angry with his interviewer: "It's difficult. It's an elusive animal. It doesn't sit in a place where you can go down, observe a giant squid, and come back up for supper."

೧

LOATES LIKELY TOOK LITTLE COMFORT IN THE poem that one of Aldrich's former students had written before the failed expedition:

Rub-a-dub-dub, three men in a tub
In search of the Ultimate Squid.
They plot and they plan,
And they hope that they can
Find where that monster is hid.

~

TOGETHER, ALDRICH AND LOATES PEERED OUT of a claustrophobic, chilly submersible's picture window at bioluminescent jellyfish, a shimmering wall of arrow worms, cod 7 feet long, and obese wolffish, and no giant squid. We can only imagine their silence.

"We had about a 50-foot radius of light," Aldrich later said of this failed expedition. "Now, how the devil do I know what was outside that 50-foot radius? I mean, they could have seen me without my seeing them."

"They're out there," he said, then pulled deeply from his cigarette, held his breath for a moment, and exhaled. "They're waiting for me."

~

IN SPITE OF ALDRICH'S FAILED EXPEDITIONS, HE considered any knowledge he received from colleagues (as a result of his expeditions' publicity) to be "fantastic." When interrogated about the nature of said knowledge, Aldrich waved his hand and replied, "It's too amazing to talk about."

~

ONE INTREPID NEWFOUNDLAND JOURNALIST (whose article sadly did not include a byline) uncovered a piece of this knowledge: One of Aldrich's mysterious "colleagues" apparently reported that he found a man "clinging to a raft with 11 other men after an attack. He survived a giant squid and was one of only three who were rescued. He was left with huge ulcers the size of English old pennies wherever the suckers of the tentacles had gripped him, wounds that will leave him with life-long scars." 11 men. 3 saved. 8 dead bodies. On a raft, adrift. Ulcerous scars. Too amazing to talk . . .

൳

OF HIS FAILED EXPEDITION, ALDRICH SAID, "THE giant squid are elusive as ever. They're gradually moving to deeper waters. On our 20-hour dive, the longer the sub stayed down, the larger the marine life we attracted became." Aldrich's sub flooded the water with red lights to attract the squid, attempting to mimic the little he knew about the ways in which the beasts flash their bodies, lighting up "like Christmas trees," to attract potential mates, or to camouflage themselves, or, or . . . (Professor William F. Gilly states that, even today, "no one knows how artificial lighting can skew a squid's behavior.")

Still, "it is significant," Aldrich said, his beard pathetic next to Loates's, his red light idea having fizzled, "that we did not see a single shark. The shark is the next step in the food chain and if we had gotten to the shark stage, maybe the giant squid would have followed them." Then, Aldrich paused, perhaps kicked at the dirt (if he was outside), or the tile (if he was in), and muttered, "rotten stinking tuna . . ."

ᔕ

JUST PRIOR TO ALDRICH'S DEATH, LOATES HAD to give up on any follow-up expeditions, forced to take a job illustrating for an American greeting card company. After working with Aldrich and the giant squid, was this kind of work fulfilling? Eyes down–emptied cocoons. "It puts bread and butter on the table." Either that's the light, or the muscles in his jaw twitching.

ᔕ

AFTER ALDRICH'S DEATH, JOHN M. ARNOLD TOOK over as managing editor of the *Journal of Cephalopod Biology*. Arnold (who signs his letters, "Teuthologically Yours") stirred a bit of controversy by moving the journal's headquarters from Newfoundland to Hawaii. He defends himself in the forepages of a 1993 issue: "I assure you that Hawaii is just as close to the edge of the earth [as Newfoundland]. For reasons I don't understand, there has been opposition to the journal from the outset. In the Hawaiian language, we say ALOHA, which means hello, goodbye, and love. We should have aloha not only for cephalopods, but also for each other."

ᔓ

AND GLEN LOATES DREW ANOTHER CARTOON-ish birthday cake.

ᔓ

JOHN STEPHEN RITCEY, MURIEL'S SON, AND MOSES and Sarah's great-grandson, served in the Royal Navy and, in 1945, after the war ended, he returned to St. John's to work at Acadia Gas Engines. One year later, he and his wife Enid Sheppard had Rosalind, their first daughter. Eight years later, Rosalind's little sister, Joan, was born. When Acadia Gas Engines went bust in 1968, John Stephen Ritcey got work as a purchasing agent for Newfoundland Farm Products. He retired in 1982, and died in 1990. Among the ephemera of his life collected by Archives Canada are two hymn booklets, several permits, and a copy of a poem.

The poem is called "Farewell to a Departing Guest," by Anonymous, who may or may not be John Ritcey. The poem is dated March 16, 1949, and is dedicated, in blue script, to Sir Gordon MacDonald, the final governor of Newfoundland, when Newfoundland was still NEW-

FOUNDLAND, and not yet part of Canada. Anonymous was not a MacDonald fan.

The poem includes these lines:

Today you're sailing from our shore,
Thank God!
Your beetle brow we'll see no more,
Please God.
Your rusty sermons will have ceased,
No more of "screech" and "cocktails" preached,
Thank God!
A prayer we raise as you ride the gales:
May the whales devour the man . . .
Another prayer as the tides ride high,
God grant you a conscience ere you die . . .
Goodbye!

ᘛ

AND GLEN LOATES DREW A GRADUATION CAP. And perhaps the squid became to him akin to some family ghost.

ᘛ

JOAN RITCEY CAN'T ESCAPE FAMILIAL GHOSTS that to us seem merely anecdotal. Thinking about that Great Fire in 1892, precisely 115 years later, in a July 7,

2007, interview with *The Telegram*, St. John's newspaper, Ritcey remembers her grandmother Muriel "talking about how fortunate her family was not to have to sleep in the tent village after their house on Duckworth Street burned, since they were able to stay at Moses Harvey's house" which Harvey himself, according to Ritcey, "helped save."

Fifteen years earlier, on the hundredth anniversary of the Great Fire, Ritcey walked the path of the blaze. It took her over two hours. She thought of the "magnitude of the event" and of Moses Harvey.

"You get a sense of how big it was," she said. "I often think on a hot summer day what it must have been like."

In this forced communion, can she really empathize with them? Why is she compelled to try?

~

"OH," ARTHUR GOUGH CALLS AS I DESCEND THE three steps of 3 Devon Row, "one more thing: Moses Harvey had a pet seal that he kept in the backyard here. Eventually, he killed it."

"Moses was heartbroken over having to have to kill that seal," Joan Ritcey said.

"Apparently," said Elizabeth Browne, also of the Centre for Newfoundland Studies, "he killed that seal with some relish."

ᘓ

HARVEY WRITES, IN HIS ARTICLE, *BIOGRAPHY OF a Seal:*

> This year a friend presented me with a living seal, so that I had an opportunity of observing the habits of this curious animal. It passed half its time in a tank of water and during the day crawled about the yard, using its foreflippers as legs, and wriggling along with its fat body in a very clumsy fashion. Its greatest delight was to bask in the sun, lying on its side or back, and in that position it presented the picture of contentment and happiness. So long as any ice or snow could be had it preferred a frozen couch to any other. "Bob" however proved to be of a surly disposition, his temper having been spoiled by the men on board teasing him and playing rough tricks upon him. On any one going near him he showed his teeth threateningly and uttered a hoarse growl. He submitted to be patted, however, with good grace, and in time, no doubt, would have become quite tame. I failed, however, to get him to eat anything but ice. In vain did I tempt him with the finest fresh

herrings and other food. He would not touch any of these; but when I threw into the water small pieces of ice he ate these greedily, devouring four or five pounds of ice twice a day. On this he lived more than a month, and appeared to thrive. How an animal could live so long and be in health on an ice diet seems inexplicable; but such is the fact. At length the April sun melted the ice and Bob's usual source of supply was cut off. Besides, he was "wanted" at the Smithsonian Museum, Washington, as I had undertaken to furnish Professor Baird with specimens of our various species of seals. But Bob could only find admission into that splendid institution in a stuffed condition. A smart tap or two on the nose with a club ended his career, and now he is on his way to the Smithsonian, to be gazed at by thousands of successive visitors and to undergo the scrutiny of scientific eyes. Poor Bob did not depart without the tribute of a tear. A young "shaver" had become greatly attached to him, although Bob did not appear to return the boyish affection; and when he lay stretched out in death his young friend was for a time inconsolable, and still cherishes resentment against his murderer.

The murderer was, of course, Harvey himself. The "shaver" is believed to be an invention, a "boyish" manifestation of Harvey's (perhaps affected) guilt.

Less than a year after he dispatched Bob, Harvey brought home a giant squid.

~

AS HARVEY CLUBBED (OR "TAPPED") THAT SEAL, that same year, the British government and Royal Navy launched the world's first major oceanic expedition, refurbishing an old warship as a laboratory stocked with microscopes and kegs of pickling alcohol; renaming it the HMS *Challenger*. The expedition sailed for three-and-a-half straight years. The crew discovered over 4,700 new

species, but this was not unguent enough to keep them from succumbing to the brutal monotony of the work. Several men went insane, and many others committed suicide, primarily, but not entirely, by drowning themselves. I don't know how the other men self-dispatched. I don't know if the drowned men imagined a communion with their 4,700 new species, or however many they had discovered by the time they killed themselves.

~

AND WHAT OF THE FISHERMEN WHO SHARED that 1874 boat ride with Harvey? What of the men with their orange slickers and ripped hands? Their blistered necks and soaked underclothes, the poorly sighted of whom having to squint through the sea-salt-stained lenses of their glasses? What were they trying to do? In all likelihood, they had gawked at the squid, and then had had enough. They thought to cut it up "to be mixed with bog and earth for manure." It took three of them to finish the squid off, though the herring nets gave them a head start. They did, as we all do, turn away eventually from the amazing things we can not assimilate.

The fishermen had tomorrow's dogfish to worry about, this breed of small shark infamous for stealing the catch as the fishermen brought it in. The fishermen had their broken nets to worry about. They must get them fixed, but how to find the time? They had their quotas to meet, and merchants to pitch, and middleman "planters" from whom to buy fresh supplies. They watched the squid for a while, hearts aloft and then, as if at a rock concert of their idol–one they drove into another province for, one for which they paid scalpers their entire paychecks–they turned away, left the stadium during the encore in order to beat the traffic home. Snapped by a squid from their comfort zones, entirely off-kilter, they rushed back into their work lives, seeking precisely what they lost–comfort and kilter–and finding it in small worry, the future mending of their nets.

Perhaps the captain, a weekend hemophiliac, sneezed small cherries of blood into a lavender handkerchief, and perhaps he clapped his hands and smoothed his eyebrows and said, "We're tearing along at a terrible pace, the jib without its bonnet–as becomes a jib in such a gale," or he said, "You don't get fogs like this down York way–come now?" or he said, "Squids is very unsartin': sometimes you find 'em huggin' in the shore, 'specially when the white whales is calfin', and again they goes off shore and you can't get near 'em," or, "they's nature's nightmare of the deep," or, "I laid back half in the water, and braced against the seat with my clear leg; for a few seconds it was nip and tuck, I makin' hits at it with the axe and missin' most every time owin' to the boat's jumpin' around so," or, "and another caught me in the hand, takin' the skin right off," or, "Boat ahead!" or, "Looks like a canoe–I reckon it's some of them Injuns that live around here," or, "and my rubber boot came off," or, "Let go the weather jib-sheet!" or, "Look out for your head!" or he said nothing, as the boat pitched forward and the men struggled to stay on their feet.

And, to be sure, the fishermen remembered first seeing this beast entangled in their nets, belching black ink; how they collectively tossed the grapnel at the flailing body, the sharp flukes and barbs of which sunk into the soft flesh with hardly a sound; how they tied a stout rope to the grapnel's assault hook; how, shoreside, they tied the other end of the rope to a tree to keep the squid, still flailing, but quietly now, the tentacles making soft slaps on the water, from going out with the tide; how they watched it as it died, keeping "a respectful distance from the long tentacles, which ever and anon darted out, like great tongues from the central mass"; how the beast went still as the water receded; how they cinched up their orange slickers; how they thought of numbers and quotas and nets and their suppers.

Even while Harvey perhaps fell to his knees, brought

his cracked face to the tentacles, muttered words like *glorious*, and sentences like *I'll take you home*, the fishermen smoked and remembered their work, remembered their children at the tables in their own Newfoundland homes upon which they needed to place something edible. This remembering wasn't manufactured as much as it was necessary. They picked up their nets and frowned and forgot, as we all do, shoving mundanity up into the crevices of the ecstatic.

൬

AN INFANT GIANT SQUID IS CALLED A PARALARVA, and it's the size of a cricket. In Latin, *para* means to make ready, to prepare, and a *larva* is a ghost, a spectre. Thousands of paralarvae hatch at once (after the mother squid lays that pearl necklace string of eggs . . .). And paralarvae are the only "giant" squid we humans have ever been able to capture and observe alive—if only for a very brief time. Paralarvae, as with other squids in captivity (Humboldt, Vampire, Japanese Flying, Leopard . . .), quickly lose their minds and the ability to communicate, grow angry and depressed and confused, and begin to cannibalize each other before committing suicide in a variety of manners—scrambling their own brains, kamikaze-style, over and over against the walls of their holding tank, or, in some documented cases, actually throwing themselves out of the tank, drowning in our air on the pretty jade of the linoleum.

~

OF COURSE, SO MANY YEARS AGO, HARVEY KNEW nothing of this behavior, and exclaimed, "Could we only capture a live specimen of our 'big squids,' what a sensation it would make in an aquarium!"

~

STEVE O'SHEA, THE HALF-DEAF MARINE BIOLOgist from New Zealand, who at his home keeps a freezer full of eggs from the ovary of a giant squid—eggs that resemble a bunch of grapes on their stem—bore witness to paralarvae as they killed themselves against his tank wall. In tears, he jumped in, and held the corpses.

"I had spent every day, every hour, trying to find the paralarvae," he said, "and then they died in my grasp. I knew if I failed again, I would be finished. Not just scientifically, but physically and emotionally."

He closed his eyes for a moment, perhaps, in his head, reanimating the dead beast in his hand.

"The dead one is beautiful," he said eventually, "but it's the live one I want."

~

"DURING THE HAULING IN OF A HERRING-NET," Moses Harvey wrote, "the live creature got somehow entangled in the folds, and became powerless."

Perhaps Harvey saw it as his duty to restore power to it, body and myth, myth and the body.

"It proved to be . . . gigantic," Harvey continued.

Approaching the dock at the port of St. John's, the fishing boat entered the Narrows, the only entrance to the harbor, which, at a depth of as little as 11 meters, and a width of 61, geographically defended the city from seventeenth-century pirates, eighteenth-century enemy "settlers," and World War II submarine invaders. Borborygmal icebergs groaned against other icebergs. Beyond them, nothing but ocean–the churn and froth of the Atlantic–until Ireland.

The fishermen were telling tales, perhaps about an old captain who, freezing to death, stabs his three dogs, dogs he raised from puppyhood. The dogs are confused, but fight, blimp his hands with bites. But the knife, bone-handled, finds its way beyond the dogs' ribs, and soon, he has stripped them of their skins and has made a jacket, excised their bones and has fashioned a flagpole which he uses to signal his distress. The fishermen were telling this tale, or the fishermen couldn't stop talking about the squid, or the fishermen were silent.

The fog that the early sailors believed to be the last

remnants of Noah's flood began to shroud the vessel, the vapors pumped from the interior's forests, commingling with the sea. The early sailors believed that this fog housed ghosts of fishermen and fish, mermaids that they'd either have to love or decapitate, that the only way to eradicate this terrible fog would be to set a great fire to the forests. At the seabed beneath them, the skeletons of two hundred ships lay unidentified in the soupy mass grave, lifeboats and their corpses embalmed in the deep freeze. The Labrador Current threw at them more and more ice.

Through the fog, the Laurentian rocks stabbed upward, themselves resembled fortresses, as if the land were battling the sea and slowly giving up ground. When the ocean attacked the rocks, the spray shattered into the men's faces and stuck there. In this spray, no rainbow. I envision Harvey wiping his nose with his right hand, his left never leaving the squid's body, which had a "total number of suckers . . . estimated at eleven hundred," and "a strong, horny beak, shaped precisely like that of a parrot, and in size larger than a man's clenched fist."

For all we know, Harvey clenched his right fist, and measured it against the squid's beak and nodded, and was to remember this comparison, even if he did not explicitly intend to, as the small boat that carried his body and the beast's body, and the bodies of the fishermen, passed Chain Rock and Pancake Rock, HMS this and HMS that, Signal Hill with its fortifications, the final battle site of the Seven Years' War, the blood from so many French scalps still decorating the citadel stone, the city inked like an ash drawing on the hillside, chimneys brick and copper pumping smoke, the cathedral cupola's dirty bowl-cut, the Battery, and Cahill Point, and Deadman's Pond, rumored to be bottomless, bottomless at the foot of Gibbet Hill where, in the eighteenth century, the city's public hangings took place, the tar-coated bodies of the executed left to swing in moonlight as warning, as display, over a pond with no bottom, into which, when they began to rot, the bodies were thrown, stuffed into barrels weighted with stones, disappearing into the maw of the earth, and Harvey may have stroked the squid as if a horse, whispered to it in vocables, and remembered the newspaper story five years ago, Christmas Day 1869, about the drowning deaths of two young girls who dared to ice skate on Deadman's, and the boy, Fred Jr., the son of Newfoundland Premier Sir Frederick Carter, who drowned while trying to save them. Moses Harvey cooed to the squid and imagined their three young bodies drifting forever downward as if on some ghost-pulley, never to catch up to the tarred remains of the hanged men.

As Harvey shuddered, his own parts shuddering within him, the boat's parts shuddered alongside—oars shivering with the bailing scoops, the bultow trawl joining its long line of hooks to the edge of the compass as if trying to catch any sense of direction, and to find sustenance there. The algebra of wind and tide undid itself and became remedial. Once again, nothing could be given, or proven. The gaff creaked like a redwood.

Harvey would have heard the chirr and scrape and whine and grind and bells and whistles of the fishing fleets, sealing fleets, herring schooners, banking schooners, coastal boats, deep-sea liners, peacetime warships, and he couldn't convince himself what kind of time it was—some hallucinatory wartime, some ethereal concord.

Confusing the air overhead were bald eagles who could have been fish hawks, osprey who could have been sparrows. *Turrs* who could have been *murrs.* There was a pigeon who could have been a Greenland falcon, a kingfisher who could have been a snowy owl, a Paradise flycatcher who could have been a Downy woodpecker, a chimney swallow who could have been a robin, a blackbird who could have been a grosbeak, a raven who could have been a jay, a square cloud that could have been a circle, thunder that could have been the sea, orange that could have been pink, and the heavens that could have been the hells.

And when the boat creaked into the harbor–littered with shredded sails, dismembered gunwales, dented dinghies, logs, knotted rope, the flotsam and jetsam of sea and gutted fish, crumb-sized pieces of which clung rotting to the net heaps, a downturned whaleboat doubling as a chicken coop, the decapitated sculpture of a dead French admiral, a boy of about nine cleaning a herring on the flat of the severed neck; a young woman standing side-by-side with a small girl who could be her daughter or niece at the splitting table, the girl kicking at the crisscross legs of it with her small red slippered feet, the bellies and forearms and chests of both woman and girl spattered with entrails; the mother or aunt beheading the cod, slitting its underside, removing the backbone; the girl expertly digging into the cavity with her small fore- and middle fingers, scooping the guts into a bucket, carefully retaining the livers in a white porcelain bowl, the homemade birch broom that they will soon use to clean up resting innocent for now against a fat barrel; a beat-to-shit stockpot, a relic from a defunct cook's galley tied up overhead like some poor flying buttress—blasting its stentorian horn, and began to dock, when the fishermen threw their ropes ashore, Moses Harvey finally remembered his role as scientist, finally remembered to think again in numbers, to wedge measurements through a waterfall of adrenaline, his exhilaration tempered with an inexplicable heartache, finally dared to look into the animal's eyes, swinging above him or heaped at his feet, and found, to his surprise, that "the eyes were destroyed, but the eye-socket measured four inches in diameter."

He considered his own small eyes, and again made a fist as one fisherman swore to another, and then flattened that hand over his chest, felt it beating from the inside, as if a Deadman resuscitated someplace within him, close enough for him to feel it, but intangible all the same, and his body felt improbably deep, as if his heart were calling to the surface from its coffin of tar, asking to be excised, to be laid into the eye-socket of this fallen squid where it would finally be a perfect fit.

ᔓ

UNDER HIS HAND, THE SQUID'S LIFELESS BODY felt not like the skinned grape as he had imagined, but like the grapeskin, cleaned of its flesh. For its body, plus the delivery of its body to his home, he paid the men $10. It is doubtful that Harvey carried such a sum in his pants pocket. He made promises, desperate ones, beggar IOUs. His hands were shaking and his eyes bloodshot, and his nose runny. His voice sounded like ripping paper, and the blood beat in his ears, and his fingernails were filthy, and his hair was a mess. He bargained with the men, one hand never leaving the squid's body, the mucosa of it holding to his fingertips, and his fingertips tingling; his other hand a fist, stressing to these men the importance of this find, as they rolled their eyes, but could not help grinning. Already, Harvey was most certainly hatching plans—the articles he'd be able to write now, the scientists with whom he'd be able to foster what he believed would be lifelong correspondences. He teetered on his feet, a collection of bells ringing in the distance, calling the townspeople of St. John's to worship or dock or table, an orchestra of horse hooves beating the dust as the squid swayed from its mooring, almost pastoral, creaking like a porch swing in the wind, as if keeping some new kind of time.

~

IN A LETTER HE WOULD SOON WRITE TO THE Sirs of the Newfoundland Colonial Office, Harvey would try to stifle his excitement over the specimen by adopting a professional and scientific tone (which included the word *specimen*), but, in the end, his emotions got the better of him:

> The beak is in the middle of the central nucleus from which the arms radiate; and the large eyes, which unfortunately have been destroyed, were on each side of this central mass. The remains of one of the eye-lids shows that the eyes were four inches in diameter. They are dark and beautiful . . .

~

THEIR EYES, ODDLY ENOUGH, ARE A LOT LIKE our own, although "they have evolved separately." And they sometimes close their eyes when they sleep, and some scientists believe they sleep on a daily basis, the only sea creatures "known to sleep in a manner analogous to sleep in mammals," and Harvey the obsessive would have known this and, in response to knowing this, may have laid his ear to the carcass, listening in vain for any heartbeat—giant or feeble—and closed his eyes, muttering, as if from the pulpit ". . . many among you are weak and sick, and a number of you have fallen asleep."

~

THERE, ON THE DOCK IN 1874, HARVEY OPENED his eyes, staring at the specimen, and felt "my happiness was complete," if not infinite.

He stared at "the dead giant," the thought of astonishing the world with his find "rolled as a sweet morsel under my tongue..."

He stared, and desperately wanted to connect this squid to the one "Little Tommy Picco" maimed. Surely the two had to be connected. "This," Harvey told himself, is "the disconsolate widow, who, in her distracting grief over the loss of her husband, had incautiously entangled herself in a fisherman's net." *Yes. That's it.* He was standing or squatting. He knew that there was a next step in this process, but something in him possibly remained frozen—some strange fear that, should he break physical contact with the squid, it would desiccate, evaporate, prove itself as tenuous as all dream.

൬

WHEN HARVEY REALIZED HE HAD TO STEP AWAY from the animal, he took only one step before stopping. **"...he buried his head in his hands and remained like that for several minutes in order to come to his senses. 'A few more ideas like that,' he said to himself, 'and you really will go mad.' Then he raised his rather grating voice all the louder."**

"Allay your curiosity, and be careful!" Harvey shouted at the fishermen, "I want this as a *present for the Queen!*" he lied.

(NOTE: The bold text comes from Franz Kafka's *The Trial*, "Appendix II: The Passages Deleted by the Author.")

ᔓ

EVEN IN THE PRESENCE OF THIS REVEREND IN the fever of his passions, and the dead, eyeless body of a myth, the fishermen grew impatient as Harvey shouted instructions to them, and to a shore crew, for deboarding the squid without disturbing its integrity. He may have thought "dignity," but more likely said "integrity."

ᔓ

PETER POPE, RESEARCH PROFESSOR AT MEMORIAL University in St. John's, believes, ". . . road transport [of the squid from the harbor to the Harvey home on Devon Row] by horse cart would not have been a problem."

I wonder about this definition of *problem*. About its nature. Its morphology and physiology. I wonder what passages of this definition have been deleted, and I wonder who the authors are.

ᔓ

EVERYTHING MOSES HARVEY SAW AT THAT harbor–the sails and gunwales and dinghies and logs and ropes and nets and boats and fuel drums and boys and girls and women and men–would soon, in a few weeks, have to be hauled over snow... In fact, the air already stank of winter, of fish gut giving in to the freeze. Of the ponderous clarity of icebergs. In this stench, surely the children of St. John's ran, word spreading, to catch a glimpse of the squid, whispering to each other as they pumped their arms and legs, words like *monster* and *nightmare* and *terrible*, arriving to find themselves at the back of the crowd, having to jump into the air to catch their glimpses of the tentacles (about which they made jump-rope jokes and rope-swing dares), and the fishermen picking their teeth with their pinkies, and the chapped red head of the mad local reverend who was speaking so quickly, they couldn't make out a single word.

ᘓ

ONE WOULD HOPE THAT, AS THE BOAT DOCKED in St. John's Harbor, a six-horse stagecoach waited for Harvey and the squid; that the driver was well dressed for the momentous occasion in a velvet jacket with epaulets and a top hat, and his mustache neatly combed and waxed; that the driver's own heart appropriately quickened, and that he wouldn't be able to stop talking of this most interesting fare of his career later that evening to his pregnant wife and three daughters over mouthfuls of pickled herring and peppered potatoes. I hope that the driver had no room left in his head to voice, or even recall, that he was hoping, this fourth time around, for a son.

As to what happened next, here's one possibility: The wind was cold. Harvey coughed. The driver closed his mouth. Neither of these was particularly problematic. More so: The horses looked to one another for help, their eyes wild, but none of them daring to whinny. The left rear horse, the one closest to the docked boat, was blond and smooth and flyless, and she gnawed at her bit, which tasted bitter, her eyes rolling back, her long lashes taken into the wind. Trembling, runnelled with sweat, she was the only horse who dared stomp her hoof dully against the road. Once she began stomping, she did not stop.

Harvey felt like he was pacing, but he was standing still. With a battery of seven men, a confusion of rubber-coated elbows and shoulders, acrid breath and booted feet stepping on other booted feet, Harvey slid his arms beneath the cooling weight of the squid's body, reaching with his left fingers to the underside of one of the tentacles. He wanted, for his own good reasons, to help lift the beast by both its head-body portion, *and* a piece of one of its arms. The wind crept beneath his jacket and ran up his back, and the cloth, like a hovercraft, rode above the surface of his body. He felt naked and infantile and light-headed and hot and cold, and a fisherman slipped and kneed him in the ribs, and for a moment he couldn't breathe, and the world turned blue, and his back hurt, and he was carrying it, with seven other men. Sea spray and spittle clung to their beards. The horses held their breath. The driver wanted to cover his eyes, but his body wouldn't let him.

To his chest, Harvey hugged the squid–so heavy and wet, and giant–one-eighth of something so heavy and wet, and giant, shared with the other men, four of whom still had the breath to cry their blasphemies. The inside of Harvey's head tried to push its way out, veins bolted from his forehead, his lymph nodes, his eyeballs. He heard something wooden and squealing roll forth–something medieval, something that had served to torture his ancestors into continuing their servitude.

The men dropped, and not carefully, the squid onto the dolly, and the wood buckled, but it did not, and would not crack. Arms so light they floated upward, his entire head a balloon let go into the stratosphere where, from that height, Harvey couldn't tell if he was in Newfoundland or Ireland, at sea, or in hospital.

It wasn't Harvey who wound the squid's arms into a lovely bun at the center of its body, but there it was, the giant squid as some dead heaving marine hairdo atop some dead heaving starlet. Together, the men pushed the dolly down the ramp from boat to dock. The beast was so heavy, it didn't budge. The horses shook their heads and chewed into their bits nearly until their teeth cracked, and goddamned their horse-gods. Someone, the driver maybe, had anchored two long planks of strong wood from the stagecoach's cart to the street, up which these men were expected to push the squid. Once off the boat, the wind calmed, and the warmth of the city and the body-heat of its people allowed the sweat to break from inside Moses Harvey, breach his skin, and encase him. He was hot, and he shivered, and he was cold. He was standing in the dirt, and the driver was singing in Basque to his horses, which seemed, for the time being, to calm them down, though the blond horse continued to stomp. As a boy, this driver would sing this song with his friends as they jumped rope.

The fishmongers and philanderers and blacksmiths and silversmiths and furniture-makers and watchmakers and jewelers and *huile*-ers, and back-alley magicians and Front Street politicians and bores and whores and the scoring and their scores came from behind their stands and offices and shop fronts and factories and basements and bedrooms, and stood with mouths closed, and knelt with mouths opened, and crossed themselves and spat and fainted and cursed and kissed and clapped. Twelve separate fishermen in the crowd bore the nickname "the Codfather." The air smelled of salt and abattoir.

A family of nine abandoned their work on the tree-trunk and cod blubber raft on which they would, in a matter of weeks, float their house out into the barrens. Two boys snuck shots of their uncle's partridgeberry wine. A woman tried to convince her companion that she was not murdered last week, as was rumored, but that she was *standing right here!* The fish carriages stopped for no one. Someone told a story about a snowdrift as big as a whale. If they weren't all holding hands, they should have been.

Four boys ran to the stagecoach, magnets drawn to the hubbub, and anchored their bodies at the street-ends of the wooden planks, wanting to help. No one stopped them—not their parents nor the fishermen nor the driver nor Harvey. That the boys would have been crushed for their help should the squid or the dolly have slipped was of little concern.

Harvey exhaled and saw that, of the seven men helping to lift the beast, four had bloody noses. He felt a throbbing pain creep up his forearm from his right hand, and noticed that, in the effort, he had ripped his thumbnail off. Absentmindedly, he reached into his jacket pocket, retrieved the white handkerchief monogrammed in plum with his wife's initials over a stitched carnation and baby's breath, and wrapped his wrecked finger in it.

With the same seven men, plus two additional men from the street crowd who felt compelled to get in on the action of lifting a myth from the earth, Harvey began to push the dolly up the planks to the cart bed. It didn't seem strange to him at the time—rather, it seemed quite obvious—that he was going to take the squid to his home. The kind of obviousness that, if questioned, demanded not a benign shrug, but belligerent scorn. If a house is a packing crate in which to hang our prettiest obsessions, home, for the hopeful Harvey, might have been where the squid is. Digging his feet into the earth, Harvey pushed the creature upward. A horse sneezed or spoke. A collection of folks began to play music on whistles. Someone danced and lost a hat while twirling. From the watchmaker, no one bought a watch.

He could hear the blood in his ears, and then he could hear the blood in his ears stop. He saw himself in his mother's garden, playing in its mud as a boy, chasing after a monarch butterfly after it had just finished mating and, in order to catch it in his hands, where it convulsed like two desperate tongues, having had to jump through a curtain of bees . . .

Time went anemic, hypothermic, and then pulseless. Harvey's right foot slipped and kicked the legs out from under one of the boys, who did not cry, and who, standing up, did not brush the dirt from his pants, and did not run away. The driver's Basque song accelerated in speed and pitch. The horses were confused as to whether to stay calm or to panic. The sky held its thrilling blue, and the street lanterns' flames did pirouettes, and the half-moon frowned, voltaic, longing for the rest of itself. The squid, as Harvey righted himself, rolled forward. Its arms toppled from its neat bun, and one dangled to the street stirring dust like an elephant's trunk, and the other slammed one of the fishermen on the top of his head, and one leg buckled beneath him and the air filled his lungs and his mouth stretched wide. From his scream, it could have been a compound fracture or a stubbed toe. Harvey, like the rest of them, had no time, or strength left, to look.

Soon, the bulk of the creature's body was aboard the bed and the driver continued to sing his song, nodding. The injured fisherman disappeared from the scene and, in turn, historical record. Harvey was covered in stink and slime and a curious satisfaction, even though the event of transporting the beast home was still in progress—an aggressive afterglow prematurely pushing its way into during-glow.

Without a *hya!* the stagecoach took off toward Water Street. This coach was followed by one, perhaps two, others—the team Harvey vaguely remembered enlisting to help him carry the beast into his house. Harvey sat up front with the driver and kept looking over his shoulder to see if the squid remained safely aboard. With this sort of load over this sort of road, with frightened horses running away from the very thing they pulled, and a driver who, in mantra, continued to sing "Ozaze Jaurgainian"–about a woman torn between marrying a lord, as her mother wished, and the man she truly loved–the world went rickety. Harvey turned from the squid, whose body collected the road dust, to his thumb, bleeding now through his wife's handkerchief. In the driver's song, the indecisive woman allowed the wind to decide for her. Should it blow from the north, she'd marry her lover. Should it blow from the south, she'd marry the lord.

Harvey continued to turn from his hand to the squid, and the driver sang as they steered along Water Street, the immigrants breaking down their tables, storing their wares and services, believing this passing stagecoach to be some indecipherable omen over which they would pray, or mass hallucination, or a chariot of the devil, or caravan of God. Pocketed by disturbing silences, save for the horses' feet in the dust and the hollow thumping of the squid's body against the flatbed, Harvey again overheard shouts and murmurs in English, French, Spanish, Portuguese, and Basque. He saw an old woman drop a cabbage. He could still smell the sea.

They passed what is now called Harvey Road, this morning's row of small girls, sisters perhaps, having long finished milking their small cows, inside now, in the kitchen, eating golden rutabaga boiled in fish stock and drinking tulips of fresh cream. They heard the stagecoach pass outside the windows, but there was nothing unusual in its sound. They finished their meal, and went to bed, and dreamt of things they would never remember.

Harvey and the driver passed the flattened strawgrass upon which, this morning, the bowlegged farmer leaned on his pitchfork, and the Anglican Church that would soon burn down. Harvey never wondered what that farmer was farming. They approached Devon Row. From dock to door, the journey was a mere one-and-a-half kilometers.

The crowd of people back at the docks had not retuned to their occupations. Instead, they stood frozen like *Guernica,* faces swirled with misunderstood rapture, hands raised in question, doomed, forever, to stare skyward.

In front of his house, Harvey leapt from the coach and thought he could see Sarah's shadow dancing like a moth inside. The two "support" carriages pulled up behind him. The moon reflected from the squid's body in eerie alpenglow. Harvey rounded the nervous horses, patted the blond one on the haunch, and returned his touch–his claim–to the squid. Its body temperature had dropped by at least two degrees, Harvey thought. He sniffed and smelled squid, and sniffed and smelled alfalfa, and sniffed and thought Sarah might be cooking mutton. In the driver's song, as it did now, stirring Harvey's hair, the wind blew from the north. That bowlegged farmer, struggling now to sleep, was part Beothuk Indian, a culture thought to be extinct, even in 1874. He was farming blueberries.

ᔓ

WE MARRY FOR LOVE, AND ARE DESTITUTE ALL the same. What can we do but slaughter our myths before they do the same to us? Harvey and his crew carried the squid inside.

In her essay "The Body," which deals with, among other things, the notion of filling in blanks, and the blanks within the blanks of other blanks, Jenny Boully quotes Plato's *Timaeus*: "And there is a third nature, which is space and is eternal, and admits not of destruction and provides a home for all created things, and is apprehended, when all sense is absent, by a kind of spurious reason, and is hardly real; which we, beholding as in a dream, say of all existence that it must of necessity be in some place and occupy a space, but that what is neither in heaven nor in earth has no existence. Of these and other things of the same kind, relating to the true and waking reality of nature, we have only this dreamlike sense, and we are unable to cast off sleep and determine the truth about them."

The sentence Plato writes just after Boully's quotation is, "For an image, since the reality, after which it is modelled, does not belong to it, and it exists ever as the fleeting shadow of some other, must be inferred to be in another [i.e., in space], grasping existence in some way or other, or it could not be at all."

The sentence Plato writes just before Boully's quotation is, "And there is another nature of the same name with it, and like to it, perceived by sense, created, always in motion, becoming in place and again vanishing out of place, which is apprehended by opinion and sense."

Could Moses Harvey cast off the dreamlike sense and, in writing of him, can I? Are opinion and sense worthy tools in order to apprehend what happened next? Can I trust Plato? And, if so, is that trust enough to stifle my wondering? Let me think. No. It's not. And so, to find out what happened next, I ask Richard Ellis, author of *Monsters of the Sea* (1994) and *The Search for the Giant Squid* (1998), who replies, "Hi Matthew Frank, You either have great faith in my research skills or you believe I live in Newfoundland."

I do not believe Ellis lives in Newfoundland, but Joan Ritcey, who does live in Newfoundland, believed Ellis to be one of the only folks who might have been able to answer this question, and, should he be unable to do so, Ritcey feels such answers can only "be inferred," and, as Ellis tells me that he is, indeed, unable to do so, he further stresses that "even if [he] had thought" of such questions, he "wouldn't have known how to find out about" the answers. In fact, most of the experts whom I've contacted on these matters either dismiss them as a wild goose chase, or point me to the person they believe to be the primary expert on such matters, the head of the Centre for Newfoundland Studies at the Memorial University Libraries; read: Joan Ritcey.

And so, following her expert advice, we can infer what happened next. As her crazed husband and his crew of seven men wedged the dead giant squid through the Harvey home's front door, which she opened, never anticipating *this,* Sarah Harvey's mouth fell down. She slid her fingers beneath her tongue and tasted salt. She heard the driver—who still called his carriage a barouche, even though it was not—singing to the moon, the blond horse's still-stomping foot "becoming in place and again vanishing out of place" in its light. She was cooking mutton or she was boiling carrots with savory. When the carriage pulled up, she was stirring a stockpot or brushing her hair with her mother's hairbrush or cinching the sash of her nightgown. She was tucking her children into bed—children who have sadly been devalued in this essay—into their small beds under which they hid their small secrets, of which Sarah knew all about since she peeked under-

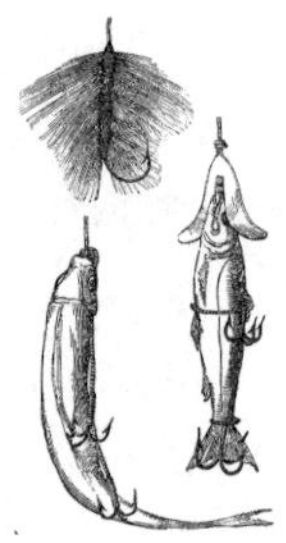

neath when they were sleeping, but of which Moses would die never knowing, too busy with his cephalopods. Under their beds were baby teeth or their grandmother's teaspoon, or a black and white postcard of a topless woman in a sunhat, or a length of black yarn, or two small found bones that were probably from a chicken or a beast likewise unexotic, or coins or tufts of hair, or toenail clippings saved so long they could have belonged to one hundred people, or dried grass or a gold stone they mistakenly believed to have value, or red drawings of the creatures who haunted their dreams or a silk and silver barrette, or a knife that had yet to kill anything, or a clear bead that was once the nipple of a dressmakers dummy, or a love letter pushed into a walnut shell.

ᘓ

IN THE BOOK *EVERYTHING'S AN ARGUMENT,* ANDREA Lunsford and John Ruszkiewicz interrogate arguments of fact, definition, and evaluation, asking: Did something happen? What is the nature of the thing? What is the quality of the thing? What actions, if any, should be taken? In order to grapple toward the answers to these, the authors stress that the coupling of research and invention is necessary, Plato's "sense" and Plato's "opinion." I had no idea until now that I may have been, and may still be, constructing an argument, perhaps, against what really happened.

~

PERHAPS THE HARVEY CHILDREN WOKE UP, BUT were too afraid to leave their beds as Moses and company carried the squid inside the house, as Sarah let loose with a string of Gaelic obscenities which the fishermen did not understand and Moses, with the blood again screaming in his ears, did not hear. He saw her mouth moving and smelled some indeterminate food, but moved on toward the bathroom, the room where the beast could do the least damage, and where it could be strung over the rods above the bathtub, and spread out.

Maybe Sarah wanted to laugh and maybe Sarah wanted to cry. The men angled the beast through the Harvey dining room, knocking against the Victorian cherrywood table, one of the three purple doilies falling to the floor to be stepped on, in turn, by the rubber boots or the oxfords or the loafers of each subsequent carrier.

The man bearing the weight of the head knocked his backbone against the gold-framed oil of the abandoned, beached sailboat, which swung on its nail but did not fall. Moses himself backed into the hutch with pewter latches that they brought with them to Newfoundland in pieces and then reassembled, the two shelved Bibles holding each other up, the shards of the broken hand mirror clapping together like bells, the twelve linen napkins, each with unique stains that would never come out, toppling out of their neatly folded birds-of-paradise stack. The huntboard pie safe fell over as the men collided with it, spilling its drawers, the fishing hooks and bobbers, the snarls of line, the brass "birdcage" reels and stop-latch reels with heart-shaped screws and, Harvey's favorite, the silver reel with a rim pull-stop, hard rubber handle, and knurled counterbalance knob, and that gossamer "reverse-S" handle. One man stepped on a fishhook. It pushed through his sole and into the flesh of his instep, but he wouldn't, due to the stress of the squid's weight on his failing biceps, feel it until later.

They passed the doorway of the master bedroom, its walls thinly papered with anchors emblazoned on faux lace. Since this morning, a corner had become unglued, and the paper began to peel downward in a scroll that Sarah thought, this afternoon, would have been lovely in shape if it didn't signify that her house was falling apart.

One fisherman stepped on a small pile of snail shells and barnacles, and believed that he had just killed a small bird. Since this morning, Sarah had swept up the sand that usually littered the floors. If she hadn't, that fisherman who stepped on the shells, whose arms shook as he remembered his own dead son's pet canary, also dead, would have slipped. When they got to the bathroom, Harvey tried to shout *Here!* but, under the squid, it came out, *Uuuuaaaahhh!* The men understood.

Sarah rushed past the men, stooping to avoid touching the beast, carrying the rolled-up tapestry her mother gave her before she and Moses departed Ireland for Newfoundland. Sarah unrolled the tapestry for the first time in North America, reeking of camphor and grease—which is to say, reeking of her mother—spread it over the bathroom floor, and dragged, with all of her might, the tub on top of it. Maybe she wanted to protect the floor. Maybe she wanted her mother to somehow bear witness to this spectacle, and to contribute to it. Maybe she wanted her mother, via this tapestry, to live forever in the first-ever photograph of a giant squid. For less than a second, she appraised her handiwork. She nodded, felt something knot and then unknot inside of her. Perhaps she felt a measure of regret that, after tonight, the tapestry would succumb to mildew and trimethylaminuria, and would no longer bear the smells of her mother or Ireland or her childhood home. But somehow, she was pleased. As Harvey again called *Uuuuuaaaahhh!* she got out of the way.

"Had it not been a labor of love," Harvey later said, "the handling of the slimy, boneless, repulsive corpse... might have overcome my sensibilities."

The men brought it inside, hoisted it over the sponge bathtub's rod "to support the mass," and stood back. Harvey exhaled and inadvertently spat onto the floor, narrowly missing the tapestry. He removed his shoes, as if he were in a temple, standing before something holy. He dug with his big yellow toenails into the thread of the tapestry, but was unable to loose it. Sarah took two shots of whiskey and then poured rounds for the men, who had to share three cups. Sarah had her own. One man cursed the temperance movement. Harvey raised his hands over his pale head and quoted St. John the Baptist, "For he shall be great in the sight of the Lord and shall drink neither wine nor strong drink."

The men clattered into laughter and called for another round. The squid drooped and released a drop of seawater to the floor, then another, like a metronome. One man thought he saw it move, as if hiccupping, and ran for the bathroom door as the others looked at him red-cheeked and puzzled.

Harvey angled his elbows like chicken wings, not wanting the other men to encroach on his space, and went to work, spreading the squid out, dragging one tentacle, then another, then another as if leaded stockings hung to dry. His hands hurt. His thumb hurt even more. He was shaking and he was laughing and he was drinking and he centered the squid's body between the tentacles, and the tentacle bottoms coiled into the bathtub below, and overspilled its sides, and Harvey thought the squid's body looked like a giant beret capping rank braids, the central button of which looked to him like a hog's snout.

The image appeared so strange even to Harvey that he laughed even louder in a wheezing kind of way, a way that Sarah was unfamiliar with, and frightened her a little; so strange, even the flies stayed off of it. Harvey squatted and, with both hands, rummaged through the tentacles, wound around the tub's bottom. He thought of how he used to wash his children's hair. He remembered the feeling of their hard scalps under his fingers. He thought of how he'd likely never do that again.

Somewhere, deep in its own body, the Devon Row house cried out through cobwebs and mildew. Some hidden beam groaned and the foundation tried to regain the air that had been knocked out of it. Moses knew: If myth is a possession, we can quantify it. If *home* is a myth, then the myth's physical suitcase, the house, must also be so, if only via exposure, as if to a virus. He knew: myth is often contagious, and thereby synonymous with want. And he knew: when we say a house is settling, what we mean is that it's crumbling very slowly.

ᘓ

NEWS TRAVELED FAST–BY TELEGRAM, SEMAphore flags, pigeon post, smoke signals, beacons, heliograph, and excited conversation. "Crowds," Harvey wrote, "came to see and shudder over it." The news, Harvey would later tell Sarah in bed, would become a *flood*. Outside, where the driver still sang and the horse still stomped, Robert John Parsons, journalist for the *Royal Gazette* and *Newfoundland Patriot*, and familial affiliate of the Parsons Photographic Studio and Fine Art Emporium (located close by at 310 Water Street), pulled up in front of the Harvey home on horseback, nine years before his own death. With him was a man named McKenny or a man named Maunder, a local photographer who, according to Antonia McGrath, in her 1980 article, "Early Photography in Newfoundland," left behind no legacy, except of course, for the photo he was about to take.

ᘓ

"HERE," HARVEY SAID OF THE BEAST ABOVE HIS bathtub, "was a treasure trove indeed . . . I knew that I had in my possession what all the savants in the world did not . . . what the museums in the world did not contain . . .

A photograph could not lie and would silence the gainsayers . . . I was the discoverer of a new and remarkable species, the very existence of which had been . . . scornfully denied, and . . . never absolutely proved . . . I held in my hand the key of the great mystery." This was his possession, his middle finger, his muse, his conversation with God. It was huge and it was intimate.

He dismissed requests from the likes of P. T. Barnum for the specimen, who later charged Harvey with catching two additional "of the very largest devil-fish for him, and to spare no expense. He probably thought they were as plentiful as cod-fish." He rejected the letters from various world museums urging Harvey to "remember them."

It was his, at least for the night. He further speculated, right then, about its love life, and furthered the story that this creature strung up before him was the mate of the squid whose tentacles were brought to him last year by Tommy Picco (fictional or otherwise) and company. He invented a relationship, a soap opera of the sea. He invented kisses and arguments. He couldn't let the story go. He was a speculator himself. In this way, I can tell myself that I empathize with Moses Harvey. In this way, we possess, we possess, we are possessed by the myths we destroy, and then resurrect by hanging their bodies, in our homes, above our heads, like halos.

~

FAMED SWISS ICHTHYOLOGIST JEAN LOUIS Agassiz, upon hearing of Harvey's possession, wrote, in a letter to him, "I am delighted at last to have such direct [access to] information concerning the gigantic Cephalopods . . . and if you will allow me an examination of your specimen, the zoological characters of the beast might be made . . ." But Harvey was too busy celebrating and dismissing his slush pile of requests. Agassiz never saw the squid, the thought of which delighted him to his death soon after the famed photo was taken. The letter to Harvey was the last letter he ever wrote.

~

ABOUT AGASSIZ'S PASSING, HARVEY WROTE, OCCAsionally quoting Longfellow's 1857 poem "The Fiftieth Birthday of Agassiz," "Alas! death has ended his labours. That busy brain so long engaged in deciphering 'the manuscripts of God,' is still for ever. No more will Nature, 'the dear old nurse,' murmur in his ear 'the rhymes of the universe.'"

~

IN A FIT OF DEMENTIA, OR WONDERFUL ASSHOLEishness, Agassiz, just before his death, claimed that it was *he* who hacked off the squid's tentacle in the famed Picco story, and not Little Tommy at all. And so the story, if not its inner sepia, eventually breaks down—to say nothing of natures, universes, God . . .

ಌ

"IN ST. JOHN'S," MCGRATH WRITES, ". . . PHOTOgraphs suffered the additional insult of fire, and documents which survived the fire of 1892 in St. John's, where the majority of photo studios were located, are rare." So the photo of the giant squid strung over the Harvey bathtub is at least doubly miraculous, a myth within a myth within a myth which stands up to the burden of proof which is, itself, another layer of myth, "For an image, since the reality, after which it is modelled, does not belong to it, and it exists ever as the fleeting shadow of some other, must be [says both Plato *and* Joan Ritcey] inferred."

ಌ

SHOOTING WHISKEY FROM THE CUPS OF THE fishermen, Parsons, whose wife's maiden name was Flood, scribbled notes in his pad in a gradually deteriorating penmanship, and McKenny or Maunder set up his camera, adjusting its glass plates, as Harvey shouted instructions. "A stream of visitors" woke their children and that night "came to the Harvey home to stand and look with spine-tingling fear and amazement at the giant devilfish." People brought gifts of alcohol–home-distilled rum and whiskey in jars. People dressed for the occasion, dusting off their best vests and dresses and hats. "It got so [that the Harveys] had to limit the number of sightseers who wanted to gaze in shuddering horror at the dead giant, and the hours of inspection." Sarah had not prepared enough food for everyone, so, out of politeness, none of them ate. They were all daffy. "Exaggerated stories were speedily afloat . . ." Harvey later wrote.

The children stayed in bed, watched the shadows move, listened to the camera explode and the men and women revel. Alfred poked Frederick (some sources rename him Stanley), who poked Charles James (who would later die, long before Sarah and Moses). They told themselves, in whisper, that the shadows were monsters. They told themselves that it was all a dream.

∾

AND, IN FACT, IT WAS. THE SQUID WAS GONE by morning. After Harvey cut off some of the smaller, pinhead-sized suckers to later mail to his friends, he tried, and failed to preserve the squid that night in his backyard in a vat of pickling brine, an attempt which, Harvey lamented, caused the beast to shrink "very much, and the softer and finer portions began to dissolve." As coopering (barrel-making) was one of the major industries in 1870s St. John's, it is likely that Harvey either had a barrel on hand, or was able to send one of the men out to fetch one. As pickled cod was (and still is) one of the more popular preserved fish dishes in St. John's, it is likely that Harvey had some of this brine on hand, to which he added alcohol and seawater, mixing it with a paddle, or mixing it with his arms in the barrel. We can guess that, after most of the crowd dispersed, tried to find sleep in their own beds, Harvey, hangover encroaching, lifted the squid from the bathtub curtain rod with the help of the remaining men and carried it into his backyard, wedging it along the two long, walled galleries that the Gough family later replaced with stained-glass enclosures.

We can guess that the men—bodies shuddering, old booze on their tongues, hands able to open and close only incompletely, arm-hair matted into miniature hurricane whorls—had to pause to breathe, dropping the beast to the floor, wrinkling their foreheads at one another, signaling their readiness to relift it with their eyes and longest exhales. The barrel would have been in between the rear railing of the gallery and the back garden wall. Once again hugging the squid to their chests, the flesh a bit cooler now, and their cheeks pressed into it, burping their alcoholic burps, feeling the acid rise into their mouths as they carried it, the men angled their bodies between the railing and the wall, and lowered the carcass into the barrel. I envision their movements as a brew of boorish and delicate, lumbering and careful. Brine would have overspilled the barrel's sides, and the men would have jumped back, not wanting to get any on their shoes or bare feet, lowering their arms, trying to lock their joints back into place.

In the coming days, around the base of the barrel, there would emerge a ring of dead grass that might, or might not, have reminded Moses Harvey of Saturn. Upon noticing the brine's almost immediate attack on the carcass, Harvey's heart would have sunk; his heart would have felt as if stuffed into his chest like a squid into a barrel. He knew–as Sarah surely reminded him–that he couldn't hold onto the beast forever. He knew that, above all, a scientific investigation was of the utmost importance. He knew he didn't have the tools for this. He was a regionally displaced man of God, and a man of science, and therefore, no stranger to sacrifice. Given the circles in which he ran, he knew of a man–a well-respected U.S. professor and naturalist who also wouldn't sell the squid out to the circus.

Early the next morning, with the help of the same men, or with the help of different men, Harvey, probably both distraught and still excited, wrestled the squid from the barrel, through the house—the tentacles dragging the floor, the brine eating into the hardwood, leaving marks that would require years of lacquer to remedy—to the flatbed of that same stagecoach, where I imagine the poor driver waking from a fitful sleep with a stiff neck, unable, after his shock at the previous night's cargo, to wrench himself from his current position. I imagine Sarah, in a baby blue nightgown, chasing after the men, wiping, with a muslin cloth, the drips from the floor.

It's likely Harvey, bleary-eyed, cloudy, having just passed through one of the more momentous nights of his life, squinted against the sunrise, the entire sky pinkening like a wound's rind, and rode with the squid, his heart both heavy and floating within him, down to the dockside offices of Shea & Company, local shipping agents for Royal Mail Steamships and the Allan Line. The clerk who accepted Harvey's odd packaging instructions would likely have been George Edward Shea, who, twenty-eight years later, one year after Moses Harvey's death, would become the first mayor of St. John's, and who may have recalled the cavernous ocular cavities of Harvey's bizarre cargo when he demanded, as mayor, that a giant clock with four faces be installed in the St. John's Court House, and then again in 1903, when he ceremonially set the clock to begin its inevitable ticking.

ꝏ

I CAN ONLY IMAGINE HARVEY STANDING AT the counter as the bewildered Shea & Company transport crew hauled his squid away, picking splinters from its wood grain with his good thumbnail, craning his neck so he could watch the beast as long as possible, saying goodbye. Laboriously, he mustered his faith in these men, and stood forlornly outside of the shipping office, listening to the foghorns and bells and seagulls, his hands at his sides, his entire body throbbing as the world slowly brightened, the birds drawing knots onto the sky. This was all he could do. Sarah held him in her arms when he returned home to Devon Row, still in her nightgown to which he pressed his ear, smelled at his scalp, ran her fingers over his back. She felt the lip of his shirt tickling the crook of her elbow, the thin skin there. When she finally let him go, he approached that bathroom empty of squid, and bathed with a cake of blue soap and a yellow sponge.

ꝏ

HE FORWARDED THE SPECIMEN TO PROFESSOR Addison Emery "A. E." Verrill, a former student of Agassiz's and an eminent naturalist at what was then called Yale College in New Haven, Connecticut, for further study. All that was left was the photo and subsequent engravings made from it, of, as Harvey wrote, "the first perfect specimen of a creature hitherto regarded as fabulous."

"Messrs McKenny and Parsons," Harvey went on, "have succeeded in obtaining admirable photographs of this specimen, which will shortly be for sale at their rooms, and probably in all the book stores. One of these photographs shows the head and surrounding arms, with the beak in the centre. The head is supported on a stand [which can be inferred from the photo to be the bathtub's curtain rod], and the arms hang down with the rows of suckers displayed, and taper to a fine point. The two long tentacles are coiled in short lengths, and hang from the ends of the rail, on the right and left of the larger arms. They are but three inches in circumference; and the rows of splendid suckers at their extremities are very distinct... The impression here is that this is a young member of the species, perhaps two or three years old... The photograph is very well executed... presenting the appearance of a beautifully executed embroidery."

The famed photo was eventually forwarded to Stephen John Hill, the governor of Newfoundland (formerly the governor of Sierra Leone and Antigua, who shunned a confederation with Canada), who passed it on to Lord Kimberley at the Colonial Office in London, who then presented it to the British Museum of Natural History.

Oddly enough, in a fabrication worthy of Little Tommy Picco, Harvey would later claim, in one of his many writings about the acquisition, that it was he himself who took the now-famed photograph. Whether this lie was his desperate and unnecessary attempt to secure himself a measure of immortality is a question for the analysts, one whose answer may require a lie of equal or greater merit.

∾

NOTHING SAYS DOMESTICATION LIKE A GIANT squid strung over a clawfoot bathtub. This thing that lived in the deep ocean was once suspended dead over a hollow of porcelain that, in order to fit inside of it, Harvey himself had to hug his knees to his chest.

This monster was tamed, but like the gods, there are more of them out there. The capture and odd desecration of this squid's body did little to slake the obsessions of Harvey and his fellow naturalists. In fact (and perhaps it was because his bathroom smelled like a dead giant squid for weeks afterward), Harvey suffered from intermittent bouts of night sweats and insomnia following the event, too excited to get his hands on his next specimen to sleep.

∾

AROUND THE GLOBE, HARVEY'S PHOTOGRAPH was immediately referred to as "a problem"—the "problem of the giant squid." The problem, of course, was that it was now real.

~

HARVEY MAILED ARTICLES ABOUT HIS FIND AND his photograph to scores of newspapers and magazines on both sides of the Atlantic. McGill University duked it out with Harvard, who duked it out with the Smithsonian to see who would get the primo portions of the tentacles, who would score the best suckers.

~

VERRILL, WHO WAS IMMORTALIZED IN THE ACADemy of Natural Sciences of Philadelphia's *Professor A. E. Verrill's Freshwater Leeches: A Tribute and a Critique*, was, in 1874, knee-deep in his also immortal papers, "Synopsis of the North American Freshwater Leeches," one of seven papers he produced on the subject, and "Report upon the Invertebrate Animals of Vineyard Sound," when a big wet package arrived from Newfoundland at his office door, as it could not be fit into his less-than-giant faculty mailbox. Verrill was a fat man with a plume of white hair combed upward into a Precambrian pompadour, a flourishing white mustache, conservatively tailored black suits and polka-dot bow ties tied carefully to hide the polka dots, as if they were a private joke to himself.

The squid was shipped by boat, likely in a wooden freight container, cushioned with a rainbow of shredded paper. Opening his package, which still retained a dampness, though Verrill states, the specimen "had been dried," he catalogs in a tapering excitement, the contents: "the jaws, which were still attached together by the ligaments, had cracked somewhat, but all parts were present, except the posterior end of the palatine lamina, which had been cut or broken off. Although these jaws had undoubtedly shrunken considerably, even when first received, they were afterwards put into alcohol and have since continued to shrink, far more than would have been anticipated, so that, at present, the decrease in some of the dimensions amounts to 20 per cent . . ."

Verrill, the only naturalist who described the squid's beak as more hawklike than parrotlike, immersed the squid (which began to break into pieces) in an alcoholic brine in order to both preserve it and lend it the pliability necessary to cobble together a restoration of the creature entire. Unfortunately, a bunch of the suckers dropped off in the brine, and were "eaten" by the isopropyl alcoholic spirits, and the body itself "badly collapsed." Verrill, in frustration, stamping his feet and pounding his fists on his desk, as if in revenge for what he seems to feel was Harvey's lack of care in shipping the beast, unfairly interrogates and scoffs at some of Harvey's original measurements taken "when fresh."

Still it was Verrill who, in spite of his tantrum and palpable disappointment at the easy shrinkage in containment of "a creature hitherto regarded as fabulous," lent the beast the name *Architeuthis harveyi*, in gratitude to his benefactor. Regarding this naming, Harvey said, "I endeavoured to bear this honor meekly. A sarcastic friend remarked that there were various ways of reaching earthly immortality; and he congratulated me on my prospect of going down to posterity mounted on the back of a devil-fish."

From these men, and from their world, much as they were gifted the same, we are given an engraving of a giant squid, and we are given the entire of its body, and both have come to us by mail, the crate buckling, and the packaging tape is wet, and the twine is wet, and the brown paper is peeling, and the return address is smudged into an amoeba of ink, and we don't recognize the stamp, and before we even open it, we know we will pickle it in alcohol, and we will make it smaller, and we already know how we will dispose of this gift after we've used it up. We open our eyes wide as we lift the lid, make a valley in the shredded paper cushion, sustaining the illusion of our race, and we move on, we move on.

ᘓ

VERRILL, THOUGH, REJECTED HARVEY'S LITTLE Tommy narrative, and perpetuated his own: that the original, inspiration tentacle brought to the Harvey home was excised without a struggle from an already dead squid by two fishermen named Joseph Millar and Robert Picco, but, as Harvey must have known, that narrative—"factual" or otherwise—was inadequate to the magnitude and Truth! of the discovery, and would have done the preliminary speculative narratives of Pliny and Aristotle et al., an "injustice comparable to sin."

ᘓ

Fact as sin.
Fact as out of our hands.

ᘓ

IN EXAMINING THE SQUID, VERRILL REALIZED, as Harvey did, that many things in this world were out of his hands, that he was limited by the time during which he lived, that he hadn't the tools to explain the giant carcass before him, that, in a mixture of sadness and exhilaration, many of his greatest questions "must be left for future determination."

One such excited question, inspired by his examination of Harvey's specimen, was, "May there not also be huge marine saurians still living in the North Atlantic, in the company with the giant squids, but not yet known to naturalists?"

Verrill was able to determine, however, that the squid was a female. A lady squid. A woman. Though she was never named, she is immortalized in photograph, and study, and *first.* After the two oldest female tortoises, she could be Tu'i Malila or she could be Harriet.

⁓

"[The truth is] myth and fable, fact and fiction . . . blended together . . ."

–Moses Harvey

⁓

OF THE RECENT GROUNDBREAKING GIANT-SQUID footage (the first time a living giant squid has been captured on film in its natural habitat–the deep sea–by squid expert Tsunemi Kubodera, bioluminescence expert Edith Widder, and our own Steve O'Shea, released to the public January 27, 2013 [when I saw it on CNN on a barely audible ceiling-mounted terminal television while delayed at O'Hare Airport, my heart likely going the way of Harvey's all those years ago]), Clyde Roper, the former

Smithsonian Institution zoologist, told me, "For me it was a bit of a 'goose-bump' experience . . . and a bit emotional, as well, because it signaled the end of an era of active exploration begun with my two expeditions back in 1997 and 1999 with National Geographic and Discovery, using an ROV and a submersible, respectively. I always have believed that filming a giant squid in its natural habitat was possible (in spite of numerous naysayers), and it was a matter of time, new technology, and resources to accomplish the feat."

And he told me, "Some, perhaps, will think that it is 'no big deal' . . . just a factor of time, money, and being in the right place at the right time, with little or no purely scientific value. I believe the public, in general, will have been thrilled with the confirmatory footage . . . 'ahhh, another mystery solved . . . cool! What's next? Pass the peanuts . . .' The general public will chalk this signature event up as an interesting accomplishment and will look forward to the next mysterious natural phenomenon to be solved."

And Richard Ellis, squid author, told me, "I was happy to see a living giant squid, but otherwise, not much changed . . . I really don't think that people [will] change their attitudes toward giant squid; most people never had attitudes about giant squid in the first place. It was a nice conceit to say that the animal has finally moved from mythology to reality, but nobody really cared one way or the other—except for people like you and me who write about these creatures."

൭

BEYOND THE IMMEDIATE HUBBUB—THE CLAMORing of the likes of P. T. Barnum and the Smithsonian—Moses Harvey's life changed little after the photo was taken. It didn't change his life, of course, nearly as much as it changed ours. As with all great game-changing works—Mozart's *Eine kleine Nachtmusik*; Picasso's *Guernica*—the audience often benefits more than the creator. Eventually, we'll forget the thing (the photo) that changed us. We'll just be changed. *Pass the peanuts*...

Harvey wasn't being humble, but was telling the truth, when he said he "endeavoured to bear this honor meekly." He was the subject of a few articles, and briefly, a local celebrity—his "sarcastic" friends bought him many drinks on Water Street, and toasted to his "discovery." He gave a few more sermons until his voice gave out. He ate his breakfasts and his suppers. He continued writing his own articles under his various pen names. He was "Delta," and he was "Locomotive," and he was "Nemo." He published them. He wrote about geography, the flora and fauna of Newfoundland. He wrote about the fishing industry, and religion, and railways, and hydroelectric systems. He kissed his wife goodnight and good morning. He picked up his kids, and his pen. He got ink on his hands. And he wrote about squid.

ᔓ

OF THAT 2013 GROUNDBREAKING GIANT SQUID footage, even Steve O'Shea, who was part of the team who captured it, who finally found his "live one," told me, "Do we move on to the next quest? Do we chalk these achievements up on our belts like some number of sexual conquests? That is a rather vulgar way to describe it, but I became disillusioned with the so-called race many years ago. [From the footage], we learned very little. We [should] butt out of its life. Sadly, Discovery [Channel] turned around and referred to it as some sort of bloody Monster in the documentary title. Shock horror. Here we are in awe of it, having spent many years trying to capture that first tantalizing glimpse of it, and there they are sensationalizing and demonizing it further for the sake of dragging in a few more ratings. No matter what psycho soundtrack you back the imagery with, it is a graceful and beautiful animal, done a disservice by marketing. [Anyhow] a bottle of champagne was opened for sure! I am rambling. The 5-second sound byte would be 'Sensational' and 'I shed a tear.'"

When I asked him what was next for him, now that

he's accomplished such a feat, entered the ranks of cephalopod royalty, O'Shea answered, "Putting it frankly I would quite like a job! I'd do *anything!* There's not much work out there for a used squid searcher that is approaching the end of his best-before date."

~

IN THE FIRST MONTH OF ITS BROADCAST, THIS new groundbreaking giant-squid footage, as perpetuated by the Discovery Channel on YouTube, sustained just under 200 comments. And over the course of the last month (at the time of this writing), two.

~

. . . AND MOSES HARVEY WROTE ABOUT WILD strawberry bushes, and codfish gills, and auks, and beaks and hearts and tentacles . . .

~

IN A DIRECTIVE ISSUED BY THE NATURAL HISTORY Museum of Los Angeles, whose mission is to "inspire wonder, discovery, and responsibility for our natural and cultural worlds," to teachers of grades six through eight, in a assignment titled, "Seamobile: Squid Dissection," the final procedural step reads, "Clean the work area by having the students put away their tools and dispose of their squid in the trash." The possessive is used exactly twice, equating, in degrees of entitlement, *squid* with *tool.*

And in the Pearson Success textbook, Chapter 27: Worms and Mollusks: Observing the Structure of the Squid, the fourteenth and final step, after locating the excretory system anterior to the heart, reads, "Discard your specimen as instructed by your teacher. Wash your hands thoroughly."

And while there were no regulations regarding giant-squid disposal enforced either at Yale or in the town of New Haven, and despite Harvey's-cum-Verrill's reverence, it is likely that, due to its disintegrating condition, the giant squid–as if at the end bell of Mrs. Ulrich's fourth-period Bio. class (in which, I admit in the name of verisimilitude, my junior-high-school self dissected a formaldehyde sponge of a fetal pig, and not a squid, the penetrating perfume of which stayed with my hands and my clothes throughout that semester, which did not help me with the girls and was far less than a golden ticket to all the champagne snowball school dances [at which Mrs. Ulrich was always a faculty chaperone, stinking of fetal pig herself], and I remember, at the end of the dissection unit, throwing away my pig, shell and interior parts, all, into a heap with the other students' pigs at the bottom of a big black lawn-and-leaf bag, lining a gray rubber industrial-size trash can on wheels which I later saw, boarding the school bus home, Mr. Dino, the head janitor, wheeling toward a long row of green dumpsters, padlocked behind a chain-link fence at the back of the school)–was chucked.

~

TOOLS NEEDED TO DISSECT A GIANT SQUID, according to Giant Squid Obsessive and former Moses Harvey Professor of Marine Biology Frederick Aldrich:

- saw horses
- miles of
  - plastic trays
  - bottles
  - preservatives
  - forceps
  - scalpels
  - buckets
  - tape measures (metric, of course)
  - knives (big knives)
- a printed description of the Leviathan in the Old Testament Book of Job:

  Harken unto this–: stand still and consider the wondrous works of God.

  He maketh the deep to boil like a pot: he maketh the sea like a pot of ointment.

Upon earth, there is not his like, who is made without fear.
Lay thine hand upon him, remember the battle, do no more.
The flakes of his flesh . . . are firm in themselves; they cannot be moved.

ᔓ

VERRILL, AFTER MAKING WHAT HARVEY CALLED "a very careful study of the animal . . . all the different organs being figured in excellent engravings . . . prov[ing], once more, that 'fact is often stranger than fiction,'" or his heirs at Yale likely junked the specimen, which was nevertheless busy decaying anyway. The remains were bagged by a janitor at Yale and dumped at sea, just beyond New Haven's own Water Street, or the remains were bagged and sent the eighty-three miles to Governor's Island, New York, to be flame-broiled by the United States' first waste incinerator, or the remains were bagged and tossed into an alley where the stray dogs of New Haven devoured them through the night. And so, this was how the body of the giant squid, and all of its mythological "fabulous"-ness, met its end: eyeless, and as dog food.

ᔓ

WHEN POPPA DAVE DIED, HE LEFT ME HIS TENOR saxophone, because he believed I would play it. Perhaps he was thinking of our two-man Yiddish act at that white piano, our bare feet picking up static electricity from Ruthie's bloody red carpet as we sang about sleeping rabbis.

He left behind, to me, a saxophone I can't afford to play. Its mother-of-pearl keys are loose, and its orange pads have dried and cracked. I was told I'd have to mail it to a place in Austria that still restores World War II–era saxophones like this one. I hope next year to get a good job with a good salary in a place my wife and I like, so I can get the saxophone fixed, and so we can try again to start a family, and so we can find, inviting ridicule, some sense of home that justifies our inheritances. Until then, I smell the thin wooden reeds. I pull the yellow envelope from the small pocket in the saxophone case, lined with faux black fur, and pick at the dried glue of it, touch the thin, stringy reeds, and bring them to my face. They smell of his cigars, and his saliva.

ᘓ

AND HE LEFT ME THE CREDO, *THERE'S ALWAYS room for ice cream*, which I've given away, because I don't want to inherit his body or his heart. My wife, perhaps in the absence of Flake bars, has adopted Poppa Dave's saying, and she uses it on me whenever I shun, like an anti-Dorothy, the act of eating when full.

ᔓ

WHEN MOSES HARVEY DIED, SEPTEMBER 3, 1901, a Tuesday, Australia held its first-ever National Flag Day, and Vice President Theodore Roosevelt delivered his "Speak Softly and Carry a Big Stick" speech at the Minnesota State Fair. As Moses Harvey exhaled his last and became mythological, Roosevelt bellowed, "Barbarism has and can have no place in a civilized world. It is our duty toward the people living in barbarism to see that they are freed from their chains, and we can only free them by destroying barbarism itself. The missionary, the merchant and the soldier may each have to play a part in this destruction, and in the consequent uplifting of the people," and the Harvey children and grandchildren may have smoothed Moses's scalp with their hands, squatting over his body, which they found that morning, at 6 A.M., in the back garden of the house at 3 Devon Row; his body that was so close, but out of sight of the bathroom where a giant squid once hung, and Roosevelt said, "We will make mistakes," and the wind blew in from the sea, and Harvey's descendants may have shivered in their coats, and Roosevelt said, "and if we let these mistakes frighten us, we will show ourselves as weaklings," and Harvey's children and grandchildren were not yet ready to cry, and Roosevelt said, "So it must be in the future," and Harvey's offspring, bowing their heads over the dead patriarch in the garden, were in the process of learning how to live based on the stories we tell ourselves, and Roosevelt said, "We gird up our loins as a nation with the stern purpose to play our part manfully in winning the ultimate triumph, and therefore we turn scornfully aside from the paths of mere ease and idleness, and with unfaltering steps tread the rough road of endeavor, smiting down the wrong and battling for the right as Greatheart smote and battled in Bunyan's immortal story."

~

ACCORDING TO *THE OXFORD COMPANION TO CANADIAN Literature*, "[Harvey] committed suicide in St. John's." His voice had long abandoned him. Some say he hadn't spoken at all in years.

~

ACCORDING TO "REDDY KILOWATT'S SPOTLIGHT on Newfoundland History," "On a night Moses Harvey couldn't sleep, he rose from bed at about 4:00 A.M. [*anchors emblazoned on faux lace...*], dressed carefully [*blue rubber slippers...*], and went for a walk along Devon Row [pre-LeMoine's, pre-*that* garage]. The front door [years later opened by Arthur Gough, the mail slot, the doorbell...] locked behind him. [He appeared frail. His ears and his larynx were failing, or had failed. He wore a robe of heliotrope moiré]. On his return, having no key, he went to the rear entrance and was ascending steps to the veranda [*My family replaced them with stained-glass enclosures...*] when he was felled by an apoplectic seizure. Body discovered one hour later in back garden.

"He had risen before the early dawn to seek relief in the fresh air. Alone, and without a friendly hand to aid him, he passed away."

൴

IT'S KAREN HAYS, THE ESSAYIST, WHO TELLS ME:

> I've been writing about words like "suicide" whose use (whose use?) has historically been forbidden in prevention and detection systems because the word itself has been felt to be too suggestive, too panic-inducing. Been writing about when what could've helped was withheld for the sole purpose of helping.... And yes, I'm writing about suicide (the act most often preceded by a vista... from the top of a bridge or a building, at the height of a chair or even a garden's stone wall). Been exploring the evolution and heritability of suicide. Did

you know that Newfoundland dogs are like the only other species of mammal believed to try to throw themselves away? Newfoundlands have been accused of trying to drown themselves. Fucking Newfoundlands. Did you know that more suicides happen in May (mmm, the tornado month) than in any other month, on Monday more than any other day? When did your Moses die? A plasmodium of suicide has wagged its flirty flagella in my family for four generations and, in spite of findings to the contrary, the prevailing method of prevention in our clan is to studiously avoid talking about it. Did you know that the guy that patented the jungle gym killed himself three years after signing the paperwork? He got the idea from the bamboo frames his dad used to make him crawl through in order to divorce his son's perception from the subjectivity of prepositions (up, down, above, below) so that he could better visualize the fourth dimension. I mean, fuck.

Just saying.

∾

SARAH DIED IN 1900 OF, LIKE POPPA DAVE, COMplications associated with diabetes. She died in bed. The last year of Moses's life, without Sarah, according to Muriel Ritcey, was fraught with "family problems, insomnia, loneliness, and depression."

Joan Ritcey refuses to believe Harvey's death was a suicide. "Had Mr. Gough allowed you inside, you could have seen the garden wall," she said. "The report on the death, anyway, said it was from an apoplectic fit, I think. Like he felt unwell and went to the porch for air. Of course, some thought it was a suicide. I don't think so. Not at all. If you could have seen the garden wall . . . It was an awfully short distance to ensure death. I can't believe he would choose that method . . ."

I didn't have the heart to tell her that the garden wall—the entire garden—had been replaced by stained-glass enclosures.

ᔓ

FREDERICK ALDRICH REFERS TO SOME OF THE years following Harvey's death as "a non-squid period."

ᔓ

IN HIS LAST WILL AND TESTAMENT, MOSES HARvey distributes sums among his heirs ranging from $500 to $4,500. Originally, Harvey bequeathed $500 to his granddaughter Muriel, later, for his own good reasons, revoking the amount: "Codicil to my will made this 24th day of June 1901. I hereby cancel my bequest of five hundred dollars to my Grand-daughter **Muriel Harvey** (sgd) **Moses Harvey,**" and then later that very same day, adding, "June 24th 1901 It is with much regret and reluctance that I have this day added a new codicil to my will cancelling my bequest of $500 to my Grand-daughter **Muriel Harvey.** I have done so solely from a fear . . ."

൜

"I CAN REMEMBER ONLY TWO THINGS [MY GRANDparents] told me about Moses," Paul Harvey, sigillographer, medieval map enthusiast, and Moses Harvey's great-great-nephew, tells me:

1. "A very kind-hearted man, he didn't like the idea of killing the mice in his cellar, so caught them in some sort of cage-trap, from which he released them into the street (whence, as my great-aunt would say, they presumably ran straight back into the cellar again)."

2. In spite of his role as clergyman, "he rather took my grandmother aback by saying that Adam and Eve were mythical characters."

൜

"THE MYSTERY HAS BEEN SWEPT AWAY," HARvey said, after the photograph was taken. I wonder if he's right. I wonder if all mystery, unlike sepia, eventually breaks down, bows to a larger entropy. I wonder if some mysteries are entropy itself.

ᘏ

AND WE'RE ALWAYS PREPARING THE NEXT GHOST, still in its larval state. This time, let's give it a tailored sheet, a wedding dress, a bow tie, a nice clean shave . . . We're preparing the next ghost, as we do with any myth, to best scare us, and define our fear. So far, *BOO!* is the best we've come up with.

ᘏ

LLOYD HOLLETT TELLS ME, "I HOPE TO KEEP THE Insectarium operating until I am 65. That will have it operating for a total of 25 years. I do not see it operating after my retirement because you have to have the passion for Insects in order to run this type of operation. Operating it strictly as a business to make money will not work. Neither of my three children have an interest in the business."

The last time I see him, he's covered in blue morpho butterflies. "Some of them," he tells me, "are dead."

ᘏ

WE LEAVE BEHIND OUR PHOTOGRAPHS AND poems and our rusty sermons and our anonymity and lost voices and Brown Bonnet wrappers and jewelry and $500 and fear and songs and headlines and specimens and sins and broken saxophones and stories and broken hearts and obsessions waiting for rediscovery and speculation and contextualization, and great-great-granddaughters and great-great-grandsons waiting for the pain to go away.

We will pass on no Insectarium.

We will pass on the narrative: sure, we are mediocre and tiny. Sure, we are insignificant. Regardless, our lives, if only in this myth, remain delicious, disturbing, and downright huge.

~

HUGE: BUG-BIT, ALLERGIC, WOOZY, PUMPED FULL of antihistamine, I weave among the graves of the old General Protestant Cemetery on Old Topsail Road. The rows are not neatly organized, but spiral like snail shells, entrap like bamboo frames. This is jungle gym, if not fourth dimension. The fog has rolled in, and my mouth tastes of some smoked salmon I vaguely remember eating this morning. That wet thing balled up in my hand is a blurry photocopy of Moses Harvey's headstone, which he shares with Sarah—a phallic pillar on a base more bird shit than concrete, etched shamrock borders, topped with a cement urn, wedged into the earth among some wayward bushes.

The gravedigger reeks of manure and has an alcoholic's nose—more burst blood vessel than flesh, a real baby's Christmas stocking stuffed with manure. He's digging up a body I can only hope is encased in a coffin. I imagine him coming up with a femur in his hand, beaming. He spits blood into the dirt, asks me, in a phlegmatic brogue, to repeat myself.

"Harvey? Moses Harvey?"

He spits blood. "Lotsa Harveys here, boy. This whole city's a bunch-a dead Harveys. When'd this'n die?"

"1901."

"Gimme that there."

He rises, is about a foot taller than I expected, the sunlight nesting in his curly red hair, the fog in his patchy red beard. Spits blood.

I hand him the photocopy and he says, "Typical shape-a headstone, but very distinct etchings. Look for those etchings. Find those etchings, and you'll find your Harvey."

He points toward the downslope. "Late eighteens, early nineteens are down there. Lemme know, eh?"

I thank him and he drops to his knees as if in prayer or seizure. Weave among the graves . . . More fog. The grasses, the weeds, the trees . . . My skin trying to rise from itself. I can no longer hear the ships, the ocean against the rocks, only wind making maracas of the leaves. Soon, I find it, and my heart quickens. I look at my shoes. They are muddy, unwieldy, dumb. They are standing a few feet above the remains of Moses and Sarah, who shares his headstone and his plot, their bones surely twining each other in an eidolic erotica both harrowing and a little funny, one mandible whispering to another, "Remember that time we had a giant squid in the bathroom, darling?"

On Sarah's side of the stone:

IN LOVING REMEMBERANCE
OF SARAH ANN
WIFE OF
REV. M. HARVEY
WHO DIED JUNE 5TH, 1900
AGED 70 YEARS

On Moses's:

SACRED TO THE MEMORY OF
REV. MOSES HARVEY LLD
WHO DIED
SEPT. 3RD, 1901
AGED 82 YEARS

Such simple text and odd line breaks. Harvey's death day, a Tuesday: four months and one day later than usual suicides, even arguable ones. Moses's "WHO DIED," receiving its own line, Sarah's wedged with the date, her death allowed to couple directly with time, her role as Moses's wife lent the importance. Moses's "WHO DIED" posed almost like a question, one that only two huge Newfoundlands can answer, their black dog-noses pushed into my palm before I realize what's happening, before I can distinguish black fur from phantom. Their tongues are as broad as my hand, and they French kiss over my lifeline.

"They're lovers," the owner says, the fog curling his black mustache, the anchor tattoos on his forearms like some parody of Popeye. I'm waiting for him to ask me to blow him down. I'm waiting for Moses's ghost to put all of this into some kind of context. I think about Newfoundlands, and wonder if these dogs will be undone by their passions; if they're already aware of some sense of drowning inherent in their kisses. "Male and female, four and three," he continues. "The male's the bigger."

The dogs piss–one after the other–on the Harveys' grave and return their noses to my hand. I wonder if they're searching for some kind of asphyxiation there. I want to ask *Moses?* and I want to ask *Sarah?* and I want to ask *Grandma?* and *Poppa?* and I want to ask after that frog I killed with a gigging spear in Peoria, Illinois, its body deflating like a basketball, and the blesbok whose leg I shot off in South Africa and the eight-hour trailing of its blood, and the broken-winged starling whose head I caved in, when I was eight, with a star of basalt from my parents' front yard landscaping to impress a friend who cried instead of being impressed, and every stupid thing I've done with my hands, stupid heart—every stupid trail I've followed—and the dogs' owner holds his arms as if twin-headlocking a pair of spirits and says, "Been eyein' ya. What's the deal with this one?" He gestures with his chin to the headstone.

I tell him, and he asks, "So you're a marine biologist, then?"

"Writer."

"Oh." He seems disappointed. "Well, there's a lot of creativity in this town, boy. But there's more history than that."

Before I can ask him what he means by that, he calls *Hya!* and the dogs flee my palm and are at his side, disappearing uphill into the fog. I take the Canadian penny from 1976—the one from my birth year that I'd been saving—from my pocket and center it on the upper lip of the Harveys' tombstone, just beneath one of those distinct shamrock etchings. I follow the path of the man and his dogs, looking for the gravedigger. For no good reason,

I need to tell him that I found it. I need to tell him about the two dogs. The fog is thickening.

I find the half-dug grave, but no gravedigger. I count ten speckles of his blood in the dirt before those too disappear into the fog.

SOURCES

Acreman, Gordon. "Self-Sufficient People: Reminiscences of the Pre-Motor Era, Building Houses, and Boats." *Them Days*, Fall 2000: 55.

Aldrich, Frederick A. "Harvey, Moses." *Dictionary of Canadian Biography: 1901–1910 (Volume XIII)*. Toronto: University of Toronto/Université Laval, 2000.

——. "Moses (Harvey) and the Living Waters: Victorian Science in Newfoundland." *Early Science in Newfoundland and Labrador*. Edited by D. H. Steele. 1987: 86–120.

——. "Sciencefare." *M.U.N. Gazette*, December 13, 1979.

——. "Search for Nemo's Adversary." *Luminus*, Winter 1989: 6–7.

——. "The History and Evolution of the Newfoundland Squid Jigger and Jigging." *Journal of Cephalopod Biology* 2, no. 1 (1991): 23.

——. "Some Aspects of the Systematics and Biology of Squid of the Genus *Architeuthis* Based on a Study of Specimens from Newfoundland Waters." *Bulletin of Marine Science* 49 (1991): 457–81.

——. "Wanted! Dead or Alive . . ." *Memorial University of Newfoundland Ocean Studies Task Force*, August 24, 1988.

——. "We Are Now in Stormy Waters." *Memorial University Lecture*, 1990.

Aldrich, Frederick A., and Margueritte M. Aldrich. "On regeneration of the tentacular arm of the giant squid *Architeuthis dux* Steenstrup (Decapoda, Architeuthidae)." *Canadian Journal of Zoology* 46, no. 5 (1968): 845–47.

Aldrich, Frederick A., and Elizabeth L. Brown. "The Giant Squid in Newfoundland." *Newfoundland Quarterly* 65, no. 3 (February 1967): 4–8.

Aldrich, Frederick A., and John H. C. Pippy. "From the Giant Squid in Newfoundland." *Journal of Canadian Zoology* 47, no. 2: (1969): 263–64.

Anonymous. "Farewell to a Departing Guest." *Dr. Cluny Macpherson Notebooks: Notebook 2.* St. John's: Memorial University of Newfoundland, 1914–61: 121.

Arnold, John M. "Introduction." *Journal of Cephalopod Biology* 2, no. 2 (1993).

Barnard, Murray. "The Indomitable Dory." *Imperial Oil Review*, June 1966: 9–11.

Barr, A. T. "The Ministry of the Kirk." *St. Andrew's Presbyterian Church, St. John's, Newfoundland, 1842–1942.* Edited by R. Duder. 1942: 14–24.

Bernard, Oliver. "Obituary: Dennis Silk." *The Independent*, August 15, 1998.

Biss, Eula. "The Pain Scale." In *The Best Creative Nonfiction, Vol. 1.* Edited by Lee Gutkind. New York: W. W. Norton, 2007: 65–84.

The Book of Newfoundland. Edited by J. R. Smallwood et al. 1937–75, Vol. 6: 225–26, 296–98.

Boully, Jenny. *The Body: An Essay.* Athens, Ohio: Essay Press, 2007.

Breland, Osmond P. "Devils of the Deep: 1873 Discovery of Giant Squid." *Science Digest*, October 1952: 31–33.

Browne, Elizabeth. "The Gazette (Montreal) and Rev. Dr. Moses Harvey." *Sources of Newfoundland and Labrador History.* St. John's: Queen Elizabeth II Library, Memorial University of Newfoundland, August 1, 2002: 1–122.

——. "Works of the Rev. Dr. Moses Harvey 1848–1901." *Sources of Newfoundland and Labrador History.* St. John's: Queen Elizabeth II Library, Memorial University of Newfoundland, July 2, 2004: 1–449.

Butler, Paul. *St. John's: City of Fire.* St. John's: Flanker Press, 2007.

Butt, Bill. "Artifacts of the Newfoundland Fishery." *Livyere.* Fall 1981: 33–41.

Butt, Craig. *Community Profile: Town of Portugal Cove–St. Philip's.* 2001.
The Daily News, November 1894.
Deming, Alison Hawthorne. *The Monarchs.* Baton Rouge and London: Louisiana State University Press, 1997.
"Devils of the Sea." *New York Herald,* November 25, 1881, 2.
"Devon Row." *The Trident* 3, no. 1 (n.d.): 3.
Didion, Joan. "The White Album." In *The White Album.* New York: Simon & Schuster, 1979.
Dillard, Annie. "Total Eclipse." *Teaching a Stone to Talk: Expeditions and Encounters.* New York: HarperCollins, 1982.
Drake, Jonathan A. "Giant Squid Worldwide." *For True Science:* Cryptozoology. trueauthority.com, November 7, 2011.
Dr. SkySkull. "Attack of the Giant Squid! (1874)." Skulls in the Stars. scientopia.org, August 4, 2010.
Ellis, Richard. *Monsters of the Sea.* New York: Knopf, 1995.
——. *The Search for the Giant Squid.* New York: Penguin, 1998.
Evening Telegram (St. John's), September 3–4, 1901.
Fichter, G. S. "Tentacles of Terror: 1870s Giant Squid Specimens." *International Wildlife,* January–February 1980: 12–16.
Flynn-Burhoe, Maureen. "Positive Presence of Absence: A History of the African Canadian Community Through Works in the Permanent Collection of the National Gallery of Canada." Carleton University. carleton.ca, November 21, 2003.
Frost, Nancy. "A Further Species of Giant Squid from Newfoundland Waters." *Newfoundland Department of Natural Resources: Fishery: Annual Report,* 1935: 89–95.
"Giant Squid." University of Washington Libraries, Digital Collections. lib.washington.edu, November 4, 2011.
"The Giant Squid." *The Sant Ocean Hall Exhibition.* Smithsonian National Museum of Natural History, 2010.
"Giant Squid Story." *Newfoundland Quarterly* 61 (Winter 1962): 15.
"Gigantic Cuttlefishes." *Leisure Hour* 1180 (August 8, 1874).
Gimlette, John. *Theatre of Fish.* New York: Vintage Books, 2005.
Gough, Ruby L. *Robert Edwards Holloway: Newfoundland Educator, Scientist, Photographer, 1874–1904.* Montreal: McGill-Queen's University Press, 2005.

Grann, David. "The Squid Hunter." *New Yorker*, May 24, 2004.

Hand, Richard F. "Preserving Devon Row Becomes a Labor of Love." *Atlantic Advocate* 66, no. 5 (January 1976): 18–19.

Harding, Les. *Historic St. John's: The City of Legends.* St. John's: Jesperson Publishing, 1993.

Harrington, Michael F. "The Sea Monsters in Conception Bay." *Atlantic Guardian*, June 1957, 23–29.

Harvey, Ed. "The Harvey Genealogist: Harvey Genealogy in Canada, Newfoundland." rootsweb.ancestry.com. Ann Harvey Lahtinen, 1996–99.

Harvey, Moses. "The Artificial Propagation of Marine Food Fishes and Edible Crustaceans." *RSC Trans.* 1st ser., sect. IV (1892): 17–37.

——. "The Cold, Slimy Grasp . . ." *American Sportsman*, December 6, 1873.

——. "The Devil-Fish in Newfoundland Waters." *Maritime Monthly* 3, no. 3 (March 1874): 193–212.

——. "The Devil Fish (Letter 2)." *Provincial Archives of Newfoundland and Labrador: Enclosures in Dispatches to Colonial Office, 1869–1876*, no. 120 (1873).

——. "A Geological Discovery in Newfoundland." *Stewart's Quarterly Magazine* 3 (1869–70): 51–60.

——. *The Great Fire in St. John's, Newfoundland, July 8, 1892.* St. John's: Creative Publishers, 1992.

——. "How I Discovered the Great Devil-fish." *World Wide Magazine*, 1899, 732–40.

——. "Incoming Correspondence." *Smithsonian Institution Archives*, Record Unit 30, July 7, 1885.

——. "Monster Cuttle-Fish." *New York Times*, September 28, 1874.

——. *Newfoundland at the Beginning of the 20th Century: A Treatise of History and Development.* New York: South Publishing Company, 1902.

——. "Northward–Ho! or, The Best Route to the North Pole." *Maritime Monthly* 2, no. 3 (September 1873): 225–41.

——. "A Sea Monster Unmasked." *The Independent*, January 18, 1900.

——. "The Seal Fishery of Newfoundland." Introduction to *Report of the Newfoundland Seal-Fishery, from 1863, "the First Year of the Steamers," to 1894*. Compiled by L. G. Chafe. St. John's, 1894: 3–6.

——. *Where Are We and Whither Tending?: Three Lectures on the Reality and Worth of Human Progress.* Boston: Doyle & Whittle, 1886.

Harvey, Moses, and Joseph Hatton. *Newfoundland: Its History, Its Present Condition, and Its Prospects in the Future.* Boston: Doyle & Whittle, 1883.

Hays, Karen. "Dear Martlet." *Iowa Review* 39, no. 3 (Winter 2009–2010): 21–46.

Helm, Thomas. *Monsters of the Deep.* New York: Dodd, Mead & Co., 1962.

"History of Lifts." Escalate UK, SafetyNet Systems, Ltd. escalate .co.uk., 2011.

Holder, C. F. "The Home of the Giant Squid." *Lippincott's Magazine* 28 (August 1881); 126–33.

Hollett, Lloyd. *Butterfly Messengers.* St. John's: Flanker Press, 2010.

Horwood, Charlie. "Squids Have the Brains." *Evening Telegram*, July 16, 1988.

"Huge Cuttlefish." *Youth's Companion*, November 22, 1877.

"International Response to Dive for Giant Squid." *MUN Gazette* 21, no. 9 (December 15, 1988): 4.

Jaleshgari, Ramin P. "Squid Popularity Aids Fishermen." *New York Times*, June 9, 1996.

"John Ritcey Collection." *Archives Canada.* St. John's: Centre for Newfoundland Studies, 1900–1976.

Johnstone, Kenneth. *The Aquatic Explorers: A History of the Fisheries Research Board of Canada*. Toronto and Buffalo, NY: University of Toronto Press, 1977.

Joye, William, ed. *The Oxford Companion to Canadian Literature.* Toronto: Oxford University Press, 1983.

Kafka, Franz. *The Trial: The Definitive Edition.* New York: Schocken Books, 1995.

Kent, W. J. *A Directory Containing Names and Present Addresses of Pro-*

fessional Men, Merchants and Shopkeepers, Burnt Out by the General Conflagration of July 8th, 1892. Original 1892 booklet reprinted in the *Encyclopedia of Newfoundland and Labrador*, 2011.

Kent, W. Saville. "Gigantic Cuttlefish." *Popular Science Review*, April 1874, 113–27.

Krystek, Lee. "The Giant Squid." unmuseum.org., 2003.

Lambert, Carolyn. *Far from the Homes of Their Fathers: Irish Catholics in St. John's, Newfoundland, 1840–86.* St. John's: Memorial University of Newfoundland, Doctor of Philosophy Thesis, Library and Archives Canada, February 2010.

Laurie, Philip. *A History of the Portugal Cove Region.* St. John's: Maritime History Group, Memorial University of Newfoundland, 1973.

LaVerdiere, Eugene. *The Breaking of the Bread: The Development of the Eucharist According to Acts.* Chicago: Archdiocese of Chicago: Liturgy Training Publications, 1998.

Lee, Henry. *Sea Fables Explained.* Whitefish, MT: Kessinger Publishing, 2003 (first published 1883).

Lewis, E. Edwin, M.D., and Ira S. Wile, M.D. "Editorial Comment: Mortality Rates." *American Medicine* 24 (October 1918): 631–32.

Lewis, Gilbert. "The Place of Pain in Human Experience." *Journal of Medical Ethics* 4 (1978): 122–25.

Lewis, John. "The Flying Set: Schooners, Dory Fishing, Bultrow Trawling." *Newfoundland Quarterly*, Spring 2003, 4–7.

Ley, Willy. *Exotic Zoology.* New York: Viking, 1962.

Loates, Glen. "A Portfolio of Drawings of *Architeuthis dux* (introduction by F. A. Aldrich.)" *Journal of Cephalopod Biology* 1, no. 1 (1989): 88–91.

Lunsford, Andrea A., and John J. Ruszkiewicz. *Everything's an Argument.* 3rd ed. Boston: Bedford/St. Martin's, 2004.

Macpherson, Alan G., ed. Cartography by Charles M. Conway. *Four Centuries and the City: Perspectives on the Historical Geography of St. John's.* St. John's: Department of Geography, Memorial University of Newfoundland, 2005.

Manuels, Millicent K. Penney. "Devon Row." *The Trident*, no. 7 (May 1974): 1.

Maunder, Ern. "Super Squid." *Atlantic Guardian*, August 1952, 17.

McAuliffe, Angela T. *Between the Temple and the Cave: The Religious Dimensions of the Poetry of E. J. Pratt.* Montreal: McGill-Queen's University Press, 2000.

McGrath, Antonia. "Museum Notes–Early Photography in Newfoundland." *The Rooms Provincial Museum of Newfoundland and Labrador*, Winter 1980 (reprinted Fall 1991).

McGrath, Robin. *A Heritage Guide to Portugal Cove–St. Philip's.* Pouch Cove, NL: Oceanside Press, 1996.

Miner, Charles H., M.D. "The Influence of Prenatal Care on Infant Mortality." *Pennsylvania Medical Journal* 21 (May 1918): 502–6.

Moncrieff, W. M. "A History of the Presbyterian Church in Newfoundland, 1622–1966." University of Toronto, Bachelor's Degree Thesis, 1966.

Moores, Neil. *History of Portugal Cove.* St. John's: Maritime History Group, Memorial University of Newfoundland, 1973.

Morris, Don. "Fearsome Giant Squid May Return." *The Express*, October 9, 1991.

Morris, Donald. "Newfie Prof. Probing Strange Squid Mores." *Financial Post*, November 6, 1965, 25.

Muntz, W. R. A. "Giant Octopuses and Squid from Pliny to the Rev. Moses Harvey." *Archives of Natural History* 22, no. 1 (February 1995): 1–28.

Murphy, Michael P. "The Coming of the Steam Boats." *Atlantic Guardian* 14 (April 1957): 12–13, 16–18.

Murray, Hilda Chalk. *Cows Don't Know It's Sunday: Agricultural Life in St. John's.* St. John's: Iser Books, 2002.

"Mythic Creatures: Dragons, Unicorns, and Mermaids: Water—Creatures of the Deep: Sea Monsters." American Museum of Natural History. amnh.org, May 26, 2011.

New England Historical and Genealogical Register 56 (1902).

"New Era for Newfoundland." *Halifax Herald*, December 24, 1884.

Nietzsche, Friedrich Wilhelm. *The Gay Science.* Edited by Bernard Williams. Cambridge: Cambridge University Press, 2001: 343.

——. *Untimely Meditations.* Edited by Daniel Breazeale. Cambridge: Cambridge University Press, 1997.

"Obituary of the Rev. Moses Harvey." *New York Times,* September 4, 1901.

"Observing the Structure of a Squid." Pearson Success Textbook. (ebook). pearsonsuccessnet.com, Prentice-Hall, 2006. 201–6.

O'Conner, Erin. "Giant Squid (Architeuthis dux)." Department of Invertebrate Zoology: Research and Collections. Smithsonian National Museum of Natural History, 2011.

O'Flaherty, Patrick. *The Rock Observed: Studies in the Literature of Newfoundland.* Toronto: University of Toronto Press, 1979, 73–76.

Olver, Lynne. "Ice Cream." Food Timeline. foodtimeline.org, 2004.

O'Neill, Paul. *The Oldest City: The Story of St. John's, Newfoundland.* Portugal Cove–St. Philip's: Boulder Publications, 2003.

Osmond, R. P. "Nineteenth Century Newfoundland's Most Important Man of Letters: A Biographical, Bibliographical, and Critical Study of the Rev. Dr. Moses Harvey, 11.d., f.r.g.s., f.r.c.s." St John's: an unpublished typescript in Maritime Hist. Arch., Memorial Univ. of Nfld (St John's), 1974: 104-B-2-10.

"Our Newfoundland Letter." *Montreal Gazette,* June 9, 1874.

Owen, Richard. *Descriptions of Some New and Rare Cephalopoda.* London: Zoological Society of London, 1881, 131–70.

"Ozaze Jaurgainian." Ysursa Songbook, Group 18. ysursa.com, November 4, 2011.

Packard, Alpheus S. "Colossal Cuttlefishes." *American Naturalist,* December 1873: 87–94.

Packard, A. S., Jr., and F. W. Putnam, eds. *The American Naturalist, Vol. 7.* Essex Institute: American Society of Naturalists, Peabody Academy of Science. Salem, MA: Salem Press, F. W. Putnam & Co., 1873: 89–91.

Park, G. M., J. Y. Kim, J. H. Kim, and J. K. Huh. "Penetration of the Oral Mucosa by Parasite-like Sperm Bags of Squid: A

Case Report in a Korean Woman." *Journal of Parasitology* 98, no. 1 (February 2012): 222–23.

Parker, W. Kitchen. "On the Morphology of the Duck and Auk Tribes." Edited by Sir Norman Lockyer *Nature* 43, no. 1117 (March 26, 1891): 486–87.

Plato. *Timaeus.* Fitchburg, MA: Focus Publishing/R. Pullins Co., 2001 (originally 360 B.C.) 40–41.

Pope, Gregory T. "Stalking the Giant Squid." *Popular Mechanics*, September 1994, 34–35.

"A Portfolio of Drawings of Architeuthis Dux: Illustrations of Giant Squid." *Journal of Cephalopod Biology*, Summer 1989: 88–93.

Power, Rosalind. *A Narrow Passage: Shipwrecks and Tragedies in the St. John's Narrows.* St. John's: Jeff Blackwood & Associates, 2000.

Powers, Shelley. "Architeuthis Dux." Just Shelley at Burningbird, June 30, 2004.

"Proceedings of the Boston Society of Natural History, 1830–1930." archive.org, November 4, 2011.

"Reddy Kilowatt's Spotlight on Newfoundland History." *Evening Telegram*, May 17, 1968.

Rees, W. J. "Giant Squid: The Quest for the Kraken." *Illustrated London News*, November 1949, 826.

"Reminiscences of the Sixties in Old St. John's." *Shortis Journal* 2 (1920): 94–100.

Roberts, Ida B. "The 'Devil' or Cuttle-fish." *Youth's Companion* 2, no. 35 (1878): 279.

Robins, Ashley H. *Biological Perspectives on Human Pigmentation.* Cambridge: Cambridge University Press, 1991.

Rompkey, Ronald. *Garrison Town to Commercial City: St. John's, Newfoundland, 1800–1900.* St. John's: DRC Publishing, 2012.

"Seamobile: Squid Dissection." Natural History Museum of Los Angeles. nhm.org, November 4, 2011.

Sexty, Suzanne. "Builders of the George Street Church." *Newfoundland Quarterly* 102, no. 1 (Summer 2009).

Silk, Dennis. "The Marionette Theater." In *William the Wonder-Kid.* Rhinebeck, NY: Sheep Meadow Press, 1996.

Snelgrove, Susan. "Conception Bay North–Hutchinson's Directory 1864, Appendix to 1864 Directory." canadagenweb.org, January 1, 1999.

Sosin, Mark. "Monsters of the Sea." *Boys' Life*, May 1983, 32–35.

Sweeney, Michael J. "Records of *Architeuthis* Specimens from Published Reports (introduction by Clyde F. E. Roper)." *National Museum of Natural History, Smithsonian Institution,* last updated May 4, 2001.

Sweet, Barb. "City in Ruins." *The Telegram*, July 7, 2007.

Taylor, David A. "What Makes a Good Boat?: Toward Understanding of a Model of Traditional Design." *Canadian Folklore Journal* 4 (1982): 77–82.

Taylor, Geoff J. "The Town of Bonavista." bonavista.net, April 3, 2007.

Taylor, Preston A. *Ezekiel: God's Prophet and His Puzzling Book.* Maitland, FL: Xulon Press, 2006.

Thornton, Weldon. *Allusions in Ulysses: An Annotated List.* Chapel Hill: University of North Carolina Press, 1961: 180.

Thurston, Harry. "Quest for the Kraken." *Equinox* 8, no. 46 (July/August 1989): 50–55.

Tylor, Sir Edward Burnett. *Primitive Culture: Researches into the Development of Mythology, Philosophy, Religion, Language, Art, and Custom.* New York: Henry Holt, 1874.

Verrill, A. E. "The Cephalopods of the Northeastern Coast of America, Part I: The Gigantic Squids (Architeuthis) and Their Allies; with Observations on Similar Large Species from Foreign Localities." Silver Spring, MD: Northeast Fisheries Service Center Publications, National Oceanic and Atmospheric Administration, 1882: 177–271.

——. "The Colossal Cephalopods of the North Atlantic." *American Naturalist*, January 1875, 21–36.

"The Virtual Gramophone: Canadian Historical Sound Recordings: History, Popular Songs, 1916." *Library and Archives Canada.* July 7, 1998.

Walsh, Nancy. "All You Wanted to Know About Squid and Octopus." *Evening Telegram*, January 5, 1989.

Walsh, Stella. "Lloyd Hollett's Newfoundland Insectarium in Wester Newfoundland." *Eastern Canada Travel*, November 21, 2010.

Wardrop, Murray. "Scientists Draw Squid Using Its 150-Million-Year-Old Fossilized Ink." *The Telegraph*, August 19, 2009.

West, Paul. "E. J. Pratt's Four-Ton Gulliver." *Canadian Literature: A Quarterly of Criticism and Review*, no. 19 (Winter 1964): 13–20.

Westcott, Craig. "Undersea Expedition Fails in Quest to Spot Giant Squid." *Evening Telegram*, November 12, 1988, 3.

"Whale Shark Feeding Frenzies Mystify, Enlighten Scientists." Mother Nature Network / LiveScience. mnn.com, March 9, 2011.

Wheelwright, Jeff. "Squid Sensitivity." *Discover Magazine*, April 2003.

White, Linda, and Claire Jamieson. "The Geography Collection–Historical Photographs of Newfoundland and Labrador–Coll. 137." Archives and Special Collections Division, Memorial University of Newfoundland, September 1999.

Whiteway, Louise. "The Athenaeum Movement: St. John's Athenaeum (1861–1898)." *Dalhousie Review*, no. 50 (1970–71): 534–49.

Williamson, G. R. "Underwater Observations of the Squid in Newfoundland Waters." *Canadian Field Naturalist* 79, no. 4 (1965): 239–47.

"Will of Rev. Moses Harvey." *Newfoundland's Grand Banks, Genealogical and Historical Data: A Collection of Newfoundland Wills.* Probate Year 1901, vol. 7: 101–4.

Winskill, P. T. *The Temperance Movement and Its Workers: A Record of Social, Moral, Religious, and Political Progress, Vol. II.* London, Glasgow, Edinburgh, and Dublin: Blackie & Son, 1891.

Wright, Bruce S. "How to Catch a Giant Squid–Maybe!" *Atlantic Advocate* 51 (August 1961): 17–23.

Zborowski, Mark. "Cultural Components in Responses to Pain." *Journal of Social Issues* 8, no. 4 (Fall 1952): 16–30.

ACKNOWLEDGMENTS

Thank you:

To all at Memorial University of St. John's Centre for Newfoundland Studies, especially Elizabeth Browne, Linda White, and the wonderful Joan Ritcey.

To the descendents of Moses and Sarah Harvey.

To James Baird of Pouch Cove, Newfoundland's James Baird Gallery for his hospitality, his cheese plate, and his conversation.

To the squid gurus who were willing to chat with me. I have tentacular stars in my eyes for you Clyde Roper, Richard Ellis, Steve O'Shea . . .

To Northern Michigan University, especially Ray Ventre and Michael Broadway, for their generous support of this project.

To that old woman with the glass eye who gave me the seasick pill on the rough crossing from North Sydney to Argentia.

To Kristen Elias-Rowley, Kristen Radtke, and especially Sarah Gorham, for their generous and invaluable editorial advice.

To that subterranean hydroelectric plant worker/ Cirque du Soleil clown who shared his ass pocket of Iceberg Gin with me on the bumper of his truck in that church parking lot in Churchill Falls, precisely when I needed it most.

To my friends and colleagues who contributed support, feedback, and often hummus and pita and beer, to this project: Todd Kaneko, Caitlin Horrocks, Elena Passarello, Doug Jones, Elizabyth Hiscox, Christy Grimes, Brian Topping, Regina and Tim Gort, Christina Olson, Ben Drevlow, Tom Begich, Karen Hays, Caroline Casey, Matt Bell, Josh MacIvor-Andersen, Jen Howard, Jon Billman, Dan Gocella, David Wood, Mike Madonick, and so many others I'm likely and ruefully forgetting at the moment . . .

To that guy with the FECK HOPE tattoo who helped me change that flat on the Trans-Labrador Highway.

To Jeff Becker, Jodi Kessler, Keiter Piles, and Ryan Shpritz for their continued, and ever-storied friendship.

To the rabid dog of Bonavista who chose only to growl at, but not bite, me.

To my stunning agent Rayhané Sanders, and stellar editor Katie Henderson Adams, as well as Cordelia Calvert and Will Menaker at W.W. Norton/Liveright, for their faith in, and time spent with, this book.

To my family: Mom, Noely, The Rub, Brian, Only Avery, Ella the Lizard.

And to you, Louisa–ever, and always, to you–for so much, but especially for making the myth real. You're my favorite.